RSC
ROYAL SHAKESPEARE COMPANY

22 JUNE - 4 AUGUST
6 WEEKS ONLY
SWAN THEATRE
STRATFORD-UPON-AVON

MISS LITTLEWOOD

A NEW MUSICAL

BOOK, MUSIC AND
LYRICS BY SAM KENYON

TICKETS FROM £16
rsc.org.uk

Developed in collaboration with Theatre Royal Stratford East

The work of the RSC Literary Department is
generously supported by THE DRUE HEINZ TRUST

ARTS COUNCIL
ENGLAND

GRANTA

12 Addison Avenue, London W11 4QR | email: editorial@granta.com
To subscribe go to granta.com, or call 020 8955 7011 (free phone 0500 004 033)
in the United Kingdom, 845-267-3031 (toll-free 866-438-6150) in the United States

ISSUE 143: SPRING 2018

PUBLISHER AND EDITOR	Sigrid Rausing
DEPUTY EDITOR	Rosalind Porter
POETRY EDITOR	Rachael Allen
DIGITAL DIRECTOR	Luke Neima
ASSISTANT EDITOR	Francisco Vilhena
SENIOR DESIGNER	Daniela Silva
EDITORIAL ASSISTANTS	Eleanor Chandler, Josie Mitchell
SUBSCRIPTIONS	David Robinson
PUBLICITY	Pru Rowlandson
TO ADVERTISE CONTACT	Kate Rochester, katerochester@granta.com
FINANCE	Mercedes Forest, Josephine Perez
SALES AND MARKETING	Katie Hayward
IT MANAGER	Mark Williams
PRODUCTION ASSOCIATE	Sarah Wasley
PROOFS	Katherine Fry, Jess Kelly, Lesley Levene, Jess Porter, Vimbai Shire, Louise Tucker
CONTRIBUTING EDITORS	Daniel Alarcón, Anne Carson, Mohsin Hamid, Isabel Hilton, Michael Hofmann, A.M. Homes, Janet Malcolm, Adam Nicolson, Edmund White

This selection copyright © 2018 Granta Publications.

Granta, ISSN 173231, is published four times a year by
Granta Publications, 12 Addison Avenue, London W11 4QR,
United Kingdom.

The US annual subscription price is $48. Airfreight and
mailing in the USA by agent named Air Business Ltd, c/o
Worldnet-Shipping USA Inc., 156–15 146th Avenue, 2nd Floor,
Jamaica, NY 11434, USA. Periodicals postage paid at Jamaica,
NY 11431.

US Postmaster: Send address changes to *Granta*, Air Business
Ltd, c/o Worldnet-Shipping USA Inc., 156–15 146th Avenue,
2nd Floor, Jamaica, NY 11434, USA.

Subscription records are maintained at *Granta*, c/o Abacus
e-Media, Chancery Exchange, 10 Furnival Street, London
EC4A 1YH.

Air Business Ltd is acting as our mailing agent.

Granta is printed and bound in Italy by Legoprint. This
magazine is printed on paper that fulfils the criteria for
'Paper for permanent document' according to ISO 9706 and
the American Library Standard ANSI/NIZO Z39.48-1992 and
has been certified by the Forest Stewardship Council (FSC).
Granta is indexed in the American Humanities Index.

ISBN 978-1-909-889-16-3

knopf

FIRST
PERSON
A NOVEL
RICHARD
FLANAGAN

The
Only
Story
A novel
Julian
Barnes

horse
A NOVEL

TALLEY ENGLISH

TIME IS BETTER SPENT WITH A BOOK

The Girl
Who Never Read
Noam Chomsky
a novel
Jana Casale

There
There
A novel
Tommy Orange

MICHAEL
ONDAATJE
WARLIGHT
A NOVEL

Panthéon

Packing My Library
An Elegy and Ten Digressions
Alberto Manguel

In this poignant and personal reevaluation of his life as a reader and collector of books, best-selling author and renowned bibliophile Alberto Manguel meditates upon his vast personal library and champions the far-reaching importance of all libraries – for individual readers and for civilized societies.

Hardback | £16.99

Journeying
Claudio Magris
Translated from the Italian by Anne Milano Appel

A world-celebrated travel writer reinvents the form itself in this inviting account of journeys to Spain, Iran, Norway, Vietnam, Australia, and beyond. Seeking the kind of experience "that occurs when you abandon yourself to the gentle current of time" he demonstrates that wandering is equal part wondering.

Hardback | £16.99

Migrant Brothers
A Poet's Declaration of Human Dignity
Patrick Chamoiseau
Translated by Matthew Amos and Fredrik Rönnbäck

One of the most acclaimed and influential voices in Caribbean literature offers a powerful treatise arguing for a newly humanist approach to migrants seeking refuge and opportunity at our shores.

Paperback | £8.99

YaleBooks | *@yalebooks* *www.yalebooks.co.uk*

IMAGINING
SHAKESPEARE'S WIFE
The Afterlife of Anne Hathaway

KATHERINE WEST SCHEIL

'A fascinating and
timely work on
cultural history'
JAMES SHAPIRO

AT THE OLD VIC

PATRICK NESS

A MONSTER CALLS

FROM THE NOVEL, INSPIRED BY AN IDEA FROM SIOBHAN DOWD

DEVISED BY THE COMPANY

An Old Vic production in association with Bristol Old Vic

07 JULY–25 AUGUST 2018

TICKETS FROM £12 FOR EVERYONE AGED 10+

PREVIEWS PARTNER

SUPPORTED BY

OLDVICTHEATRE.COM

PRINCIPAL PARTNER

pwc

THE OLD VIC ENDOWMENT TRUST

Bristol Old Vic

RBC

Royal Bank of Canada

DONMAR®

THE WAY OF THE WORLD

BY WILLIAM CONGREVE

29 MARCH - 26 MAY 2018

CAST

FISAYO AKINADE | ALEX BECKETT | GABRIELLE BROOKS | PHOEBE FRANCES BROWN
HAYDN GWYNNE | SARAH HADLAND | JENNY JULES | SIMON MANYONDA
CAROLINE MARTIN | TOM MISON | JUSTINE MITCHELL | CHRISTIAN PATTERSON
GEOFFREY STREATFEILD | NATHAN WELSH

DIRECTOR **JAMES MACDONALD**
DESIGNER **ANNA FLEISCHLE**
LIGHTING DESIGNER **PETER MUMFORD**
SOUND DESIGNER AND COMPOSER **MAX PAPPENHEIM**
MOVEMENT DIRECTOR **FRANCINE WATSON COLEMAN**

Photo by Eivind Hansen

ADDITIONAL TICKETS RELEASED ON MONDAYS AT NOON

DONMARWAREHOUSE.COM
020 3282 3808

Supported using public funding by
ARTS COUNCIL
ENGLAND

Celebrating **10 YEARS** of partnership
♦ BARCLAYS

Charmed lives in Greece Ghika, Craxton, Leigh Fermor

Art, literature and friendships in Greece

Until 15 July

Free

Nikos Hadjikyriakos-Ghika (1906–1994), *Study for a poster*. Tempera on cardboard, 1948. Benaki Museum – Ghika Gallery, Athens. © Benaki Museum 2018.

Supported by

THE A. G. LEVENTIS FOUNDATION

Organised with

A. G. Leventis Gallery

In collaboration with
the Benaki Museum and
the Craxton Estate

CONTENTS

Introduction

'You couldn't make it up', people keep saying, watching news bulletins flash across screens. The political world seems to be turning into fiction, with unexpectedly dramatic and bewildering plots and subplots. By contrast, in this issue of *Granta* we try to disentangle theatre and politics, and remember that acts have consequences, and that those consequences, while not always predictable, are rarely surprising.

In 'Days of Awe', A.M. Homes considers questions of desire and authorial legitimacy with her trademark humour and insight – her main protagonist has written a novel about the multi-generational effects of Holocaust trauma, and is attending a conference on genocide. The delicate question of who owns the story of the Shoah is woven into satire. Homes is so good on popular culture, ranging from conference questions to corporate sponsorship (SOMETIMES GETTING HAPPY SHOULD BE SIMPLE reads the slogan on a chocolate bar wrapper advertising antidepressants). Gerda Hoff, an elderly Holocaust survivor, confronts the nameless novelist. 'You want to know what I like?' she says. 'Chocolate ice cream. That's something to live for. Your book, *a shaynem dank dir im pupik*. I lived it, I don't have to read it.'

A shaynem dank dir im pupik: Yiddish for 'many thanks to your belly button', or: thanks for nothing.

Joshua Cohen's surreal story 'Mall Camp, Seasons 1 & 2' shows a Syrian boy mapping his lost cultural logic onto the crumbling colour-coded edifice of his new world; a closed refugee camp located in an unfinished shopping mall in Greece. This too is a story about the aftermath of violence, but in this case the trauma is so recent that its discourse and even its language is as yet unformed.

In this issue we are publishing Malaysian-Chinese author Ho Sok Fong for the first time in English. Her short story is about teaching in the context of censorship and conservative Islamic forces. Staff at the school are let go for slight indiscretions or infringements of the rules and disappear quietly into other lives. The story has an eerie, almost dystopian, quality – the acts are subtle; the consequences fundamental and inescapable.

We commissioned Russian author Sana Valiulina to write a memoir piece about her father, who was a Gulag prisoner. 'Root and Branch', written in dense and lyrical prose, translated by Polly Gannon, describes a tour of Perm, stopping to see sights including a derelict prison camp and museum. Valiulina's father was captured by the Nazis in 1942, and transferred to a British POW camp after the war, from which he was deported to the Soviet Union. I have read many descriptions of the Gulag from the Soviet era, but this is a contemporary view, a landscape dotted with new churches and billboards of Christian messages, where the memory of the huge punitive machinery of the camps is discouraged or even repressed. What is left? Barbed wire and timber huts, gradually sinking into the Earth.

We also commissioned reporter Charles Glass and the eminent photographer Don McCullin to travel to Palmyra in Syria. In 2015 ISIS troops murdered Khaled Assa'ad, archaeologist and Palmyra's head of antiquities, and ravaged the ruins. The question is the same: what is left now? Some of the ruins are still standing, but much has been destroyed. The most poignant description, perhaps, is of the silence in Tadmor, the town outside Palmyra. Before the war it had a population of some 70,000 people. Last autumn, barely a hundred people remained.

We have two reports from Britain in this issue. Jason Cowley, a former editor of *Granta* who now edits the *New Statesman*, returns to his home town of Harlow to investigate the death of Polish immigrant Arkadiusz Jozwik. On the night of 27 August 2016, a group of teenagers came across Jozwik and some friends who were eating pizza from a local takeaway. Insults were traded and Jozwik was punched, fell, and hit his head. He later died in hospital. It's a simple and tragic story, but in the context of Brexit the narrative mutated until it was cited as evidence of English anti-European discrimination and hatred. Essex police were the first to suggest this: the death was a potential hate crime, they said. The Polish president wrote to religious leaders urging them to help prevent xenophobic attacks; the ambassador was taken on a tour of Harlow, and, astonishingly, Polish police officers were sent to patrol the area.

Our second report is from London. There are not many independent shops left on British high streets. Their disappearance is not a mystery – high business rates and rents, and competition from chains, have forced them out. The only shops exempt from punitive rates are charity shops, which is partly why they have become such a significant (and somewhat depressing) feature of our towns. Councils could create more subtle and dynamic policies that would make for more diversity on our high streets – as it is we are stuck with shops that are generic and dull, a race to the bottom in terms of town planning. David Flusfeder visits some of the most unique shops that remain in London, but his narrative is not just about the shops – it's also about the people who own and run them. He notes their expertise; their ability to measure you up with a glance, see what you are made of. It's a portrait of old London, fragments of which still persist, despite everything.

Finally, we are publishing a series of Edward Burtynsky's extraordinary photographs of scarred landscapes. Various forms of development have spread like a disease on the skin of the Earth. 'Burtynsky shows us suburbia pressed against wetlands, supertanker graveyards in Bangladesh and parking lots so big they challenge comprehension,' Anthony Doerr writes in his introduction to the photoessay. 'His best photographs are expressionistic, almost calligraphic, as though he's displaying the hidden signatures our collective appetites have etched across the Earth. They are startling, frozen pictures, sometimes remote, sometimes intimate, sometimes both at the same time.'

'Look at this, the pictures say. See this. This is happening. This is where you live.' ∎

Sigrid Rausing

ARVON

COURSES & RETREATS 2018

WORKSHOPS | ONE-TO-ONE TUTORIALS
TIME AND SPACE TO WRITE

HOME OF CREATIVE WRITING

TUTORS INCLUDE:

INUA ELLAMS • MARK HADDON • KAREN MCCARTHY WOOLF
JOELLE TAYLOR • LOIS PRYCE • TANIKA GUPTA • DAVID QUANTICK
CHRIS THORPE • DAVID ELDRIDGE • ALEXIS ZEGERMAN • PETER SANSOM
NIKESH SHUKLA • KEI MILLER • KATHRYN WILLIAMS • MELISSA BENN

Book now at www.arvon.org

© HAROLD EDGERTON / MIT
Bullet through apple, 1964
Courtesy of Palm Press, Inc.

DAYS OF AWE

A.M. Homes

He is the War Correspondent, she is the Transgressive Novelist. They have been flown in for the summit on Genocide(S). She spots him at the airport baggage claim and nods in the direction of a student holding up a legal pad with his name written on it in heavy black marker – misspelled.

'Want to share my ride?' he asks.

Caught off guard, she shakes her head no.

She doesn't want anyone picking her up, doesn't want the obligation to entertain the young student/fan/retired teacher/ part-time real-estate broker for the forty-five minutes it takes to get where they're going.

Every time she says yes to these things – conferences, readings, guest lectures – it's because she hasn't learned to say no. And she has the misguided fantasy that time away from home will allow her to think, to get something done. She has brought work with her: the short story she can't crack, the novel she's supposed to finish, the friend's book that needs a blurb, last Sunday's newspaper . . .

'Nice to see you,' the man at the car-rental place says, even though they've never met. He gives her the keys to a car with New Hampshire plates, LIVE FREE OR DIE. She drives north toward the small college town where experts in torture politics, murder, along with neuroscientists, academics, survivors, and a few 'special guests' will convene in what's become an ongoing attempt to make sense of it all, as though such a thing were possible.

It is September, and despite her having been out of school for decades, the academic calendar still exerts its pull; she's filled with the desire for new beginnings. It is the season of bounty; the apple trees are heavy with fruit, the wild grass along the highway is high. Wind sweeps through the trees. Everything breathes deeply, nature's end-of-summer sigh. In a couple of hours, a late-afternoon thunderstorm will sweep through, rinsing the air clean.

The town has climbed out of a depression by branding itself, 'America's Hometown'. Flags fly from the lampposts. Signs announce the autumn harvest celebration, a film festival, and a chamber-music series at the Presbyterian church.

She parks behind the conference center and slips in through the employee entrance and down the long hall to a door marked THIS WAY TO LOBBY.

On the wall is a full-length mirror with a handwritten message on the glass: CHECK YOUR SMILE AND ASK YOURSELF, AM I READY TO SERVE?

The War Correspondent comes through the hotel's front door at the same time as she slides in through the unmarked door by the registration desk.

'Funny seeing you here,' he says.

'Is it?'

He stands at the reception desk. The thick curls that he long ago kept short are receding; in compensation they're longer and more unruly.

He makes her uncomfortable, uncharacteristically shy.

She wonders how he looks so good. She glances down. Her linen blouse is heavily wrinkled, while his shirt is barely creased.

The receptionist hands him an important-looking envelope from FedEx.

She's given a heavily taped brown box and a copy of the conference schedule.

'What did you get?' she asks as he's opening the FedEx.

'Galleys of a magazine piece,' he says. 'You?'

She shakes the box. 'Cracker Jacks?'

He laughs.

She glances down at the schedule. 'We're back-to-back at the opening ceremonies.'

'What time is the first event?'

'Twelve thirty.' She thinks of these things as marathons; pacing is everything. 'You've got an hour.'

'I was hoping to take a shower,' he says.

'Your room's not quite ready,' the receptionist tells him.

'Did you fly in from a war zone?' she asks.

'Washington,' he says. 'There was a Press Club dinner last night, and I was in Geneva the day before, and before that the war.'

'Quite a slide from there to here,' she says.

'Not really,' he says. 'No matter how nice the china, it's still a rubber chicken.'

The receptionist clicks the keys until she locates a room that's ready. 'I found you a lovely room. You'll be very happy.' She hands him the key card. 'You're both on the executive floor.'

'Dibs on the cheese cubes,' he says.

She knew him long ago before either of them had become anyone. They were part of a group, fresh out of college, working in publishing, that met regularly at a bar. He was deeply serious, a permanently furrowed brow, and he was married – that was the funny thing, and they all talked about it behind his back. Who was married at twenty-three? No one ever saw the wife – that's what they called her. Even now she doesn't know the woman's name.

An older man approaches the War Correspondent. 'Very big fan,' the man says, resting his hand on the Correspondent's shoulder. 'I have a story for you about a trip my wife and I went on.' He pauses, clears his throat. 'We were in Germany and decided to visit the camps. When we got to our hotel, I asked, "How do we get there?" They tell us take a train and then a bus, and when you arrive, there will be someone there to lead you. We go, it's terrifying; all I can think of as the train goes clackety-clack is that these are the same rails that took my family away. We get to the camp, there's a cafe and a bookstore selling postcards – we don't know what to think. And when we get back to the hotel, the young German girl at the front desk looks at us with a big smile and says, "Did you enjoy your visit to Dachau?" Do we laugh or cry?' The man pauses. 'So what do you think?'

The War Correspondent nods. 'It's hard to know, isn't it?'

'We did both,' the man says. 'We laughed, we cried, and we're never going back.'

The Correspondent catches her eye and smiles. There are delightful creases by his eyes that weren't there years ago.

She's annoyed. Why is his smile so quick, so perfect?

As she moves toward the elevator, a conference volunteer catches her arm. 'Don't forget your welcome bag.' The volunteer hands her a canvas tote, laden with genocide swag.

She goes straight to her room, puts the DO NOT DISTURB sign on the door, and locks it. What is his room like? Is it the same size, one window overlooking the parking lot? Or is it bigger? Is it a suite with an ocean view? They're hundreds of miles from the sea. Is there a hierarchy to Genocide(S) housing?

'Do you ever go off-duty?' she hears her therapist's voice asking.

Not really.

She unpacks the welcome bag: a coffee mug from the local college, a notepad and pen from a famous card company – WHEN YOU CAN'T FIND WORDS, LET US SPEAK FOR YOU – and a huge bar of chocolate from a pharmaceutical company that makes a popular antidepressant. The wrapper reads SOMETIMES GETTING HAPPY SHOULD BE SIMPLE.

She thinks of her therapist. She has the opposite of transference – she never wishes the therapist were her mother or her lover. She thinks of the therapist and is relieved not to be married or related to her. A decision as small as trying to decide where to go for dinner or what to eat would take hours of negotiation and processing. Eventually she would cave in and do whatever she had to to make it stop. She secretly thinks the therapist is a passive-aggressive bully and perhaps should have been a lawyer.

'You wrote an exceptionally strong book illustrating the multi-generational effects of Holocaust trauma. You knew there would be questions.' She hears the therapist's voice loud and clear in her head.

'It's a novel. I made it up.'

'You created the characters, but the emotional truths are very real. There are different kinds of knowing.'

Silence.

'You spent years inhabiting the experience on every level – remember when you starved yourself? When you drank tainted water? When you didn't bathe for thirty days?'

'Yes, but I was not in the Holocaust. I am an impostor – the critics made that quite clear.'

The therapist clucks and shakes her head.

The Novelist wonders, aren't therapists trained not to cluck?

'Critics aren't the same as readers, and your readers felt you gave language and illumination to a very difficult aspect of their experience. And you won an international award.' The therapist pauses. 'I find it interesting that you have to do this.'

'Do what?'

'Undermine yourself.'

'Because I'm better at it than anyone?' She glances up, smiling.

The therapist has the sad face on.

'At least I'm honest,' she says.

Still the sad face.

'Really?' she asks.

'Really,' the therapist says.

S he said yes to the Genocide(S) conference after having made a pact with herself to say no to everything, a move toward getting back to work on a new book. She'd spent the better part of a year on a book tour, traveling the world giving readings, doing interviews, answering questions that felt like interrogations. It was as if the journalists thought that by asking often enough and in enough languages, eventually something would fall out, some admission, some other story – but in fact there was nothing more. She'd put it all in the book.

In the hotel-room mirror, she takes a look at herself. 'Check your smile and ask yourself, Am I ready to serve?'

She blushes. She was thinking about him – the War Correspondent.

Her phone rings.

'Are you there yet?' Lisa asks. 'I wanted to make sure you arrived safely.'

'I'm fine,' she says.

'Did you get the box?'

'I think so,' she says.

'Did you open it?'

'No.'

'Well, go ahead.'

She doesn't open the box, just the note on top: *Sorry we fought. Here's making it up to you ...*

'But we didn't fight,' she says.

'I know, but we usually do, and I had to order it ten days in advance,' Lisa says.

'You could have tried a little harder,' she says.

'What do you mean?' Lisa says. 'I planned the whole thing weeks ago.'

'I mean you could have at least picked the fight if you knew you'd already sent a make-up gift,' she says.

'I don't get you,' Lisa says. 'I really don't.'

'I'm joking. You're taking it way too literally.'

'Now you're criticizing me?'

'Never mind,' she says. 'Thank you. You know I love chocolate.'

'Indeed I do,' Lisa says, not realizing that the Novelist hasn't even opened the box.

She knows Lisa well enough to know exactly what's in the box. Instead she opens the chocolate bar sponsored by the antidepressant manufacturer and takes a big bite. The thick sound of chocolate being chewed fills air.

'That's more like it,' Lisa says.

'I have to go,' she says. 'I'm just getting to the check-in desk.' She looks at herself in the mirror; can Lisa tell when she's lying?

'What is going on with you?' Lisa says. 'I can't read you.'

'Ignore me,' she says. 'I'm lost in thought.'

'I'll find you later,' Lisa says, hanging up.

The welcome lunch is served: cold salads like the sisterhood lunch after a bar mitzvah, a trio of scoops, egg salad, tuna salad, potato salad, a roll and butter, coffee or tea.

She is seated at the head table among the academics with university appointments in the fields of trauma and tragedy. The War Correspondent is two seats down.

The man she wants to meet, Otto Hauser, the ephemerologist, is missing. His seat is empty. His plate is marked VEGAN.

'Has anyone seen Otto Hauser?' she asks repeatedly. She has been obsessed with Otto Hauser for years, having read the only two interviews he's ever given and seen a glimpse of him in a documentary. She heard later that he asked to have himself taken out of the picture.

Finally someone tells her that Otto has been delayed; there was a fire in his warehouse near Munich.

The conference leader, himself the victim of a violent attack that left him with only half a tongue, calls the room to order. It is difficult to understand what he's saying. She finds herself looking for clues from the deaf interpreter on the far side of the stage.

'This year's program, From Genocide(S) to Generosity: Toward a New Understanding, brings together diverse communities, including but not limited to Cambodia, East Timor, Rwanda, the Sudan, the former Yugoslavia, the Holocaust of World War II, the history of colonial genocides, and the early response to the Aids epidemic. And this weekend we ask the important question: Why? Why do Genocide(S) continue to happen?'

He goes on to thank their sponsors, an airline, two global search engines, an insurance firm, the already mentioned antidepressant manufacturer, and a family-owned ice-cream company.

Before turning the microphone over to a fellow board member, he says, 'The cash bar in the Broadway Suite will be open until midnight and serving complimentary fresh juices donated by Be My Squeeze, and this year we have a spiritual recharge room for meditation or prayer with the bonus of a free chair massage brought to us by Watch Your Back.'

Following the conference leader's welcome, the chair of the local English department does the honors, introducing her. The chair's words are passionate and strange, a simultaneous celebration and denigration of her, both personally and professionally. All in the same breath, the chair mentions the author's being known for her lusciously thick dark hair, that she won France's Nyssen Prize for International Literature, and what a shock it was to her that the book had sold so many copies.

The War Correspondent leans across and whispers loudly over heads, 'I think she wants to fuck you.'

'I feel like she just did,' she whispers back before standing and taking the microphone briefly. 'Thank you, Professor,' she says, intentionally calling the woman 'Professor' rather than 'Chair'. 'You clearly know more about me than I know about myself.'

There is laughter in the house.

The War Correspondent is introduced by the college's football coach. '*When Dirt and Blood Mix* is Eric Bitterberg's very personal story of being on the front lines with his best friend from high school, a US Army sergeant.'

'Is it Biter-berg or Bitter-berg?' she whispers loudly in his direction.

'Depends on my mood,' he says.

The afternoon session immediately follows lunch. While others go off to sessions such as Australia's Stolen Generations and The Killing Fields Revisited, she heads toward the Americas Suite for her first panel, Where I'm Calling From: Modern Germany and Related His/Her Stories.

Her fellow panelists include a young German scholar who, despite being fluent in English insists on speaking in German, and Gerda Hoff, an elderly local woman who survived the camps and more recently cancer and has now written a memoir, called *Living to Live*.

'You look different than the photo on your book,' the moderator says as she sits down – it's not a compliment.

And then, without a beat, the moderator begins: 'Germany and family history – where was your family during the Holocaust?'

The German panelist says that his grandparents were in the food business and struggled.

'They were butchers,' the moderator says; it's not a question but a statement.

'Yes,' the German confirms, and declines to say more.

The survivor says her father was a teacher and her mother was a woman known for her beautiful voice. She and her siblings watched as her parents were shot in the back and fell into large open graves. She is the only one still alive; her sisters died in the camps, and two years ago her brother jumped in front of a train.

'And you?'

The Novelist would like to buy a vowel. She'd like to pass, to simply evaporate, or at least have someone explain that clearly there was an error in putting these panels together, because she doesn't belong here.

She draws a breath and allows for the weight of the air to settle before she explains: Her family wasn't from Germany but rather Latvia. They arrived in America before the war, and were dairy farmers in New England.

It's like she's on a quiz show with points awarded for the most authentic answer. She's plainly the loser.

She scans the audience. There are no young people. It reminds her of the classical concerts her parents used to take her to; no matter how old she got, she was always the youngest one.

The moderator carries on. At some point, while her mind is elsewhere, the conversation turns back to her, with the question, 'Is there such a thing as Holocaust fiction? Are there experiences where the facts of history are already so challenged that we dare not fictionalize them?'

She takes a moment, then leans forward in her chair, drawing the microphone close, unnecessary considering the size of the room. This is the question asked around the world, the moment they've all been waiting for.

'Yes,' she says definitively, and then pauses. 'Yes, there is such a thing as Holocaust fiction. It's not something I invented. There are many novels that are set during or relate to the Holocaust, including books by Elie Wiesel, Thomas Keneally, Bernhard Schlink, and so on. With regard to the question "Are some subjects so historically sensitive that we shouldn't touch them in fiction?" I'd say the purpose of fiction is to illustrate and illuminate. We see ourselves more clearly through the stories we tell.'

'But what is your relation to the Holocaust?' the moderator drills down.

'I am a Jew, my grandfather's brothers died in the camps.'

'What does it mean to you to be a transgressive woman who writes books that are intentionally shocking?'

' "Transgressive" is a word you use to describe me; it's what you label me to make me other than you. The very history we are here to discuss reminds us of the danger of labels and separating people into categories.'

Throughout the audience there are murmurs of approval. Despite the fact that these panels are supposed to be conversations, they are actually competitions, judged by the audience. 'As for the question regarding an intention to shock, I have written nothing that didn't first appear in the morning paper,' she says, aware that she's got a week-old paper in her bag right now. 'What is truly shocking is how little we do to prevent these things from happening again and –'

'Fiction is a luxury our families didn't have,' Gerda Hoff cuts her off. 'We didn't pack our summer reading and go off to the camps, happy, happy. This isn't even your story. What right do you have to be telling it? It is insulting. I am one little old lady, but I am here representing six million Jews who cannot speak for themselves.'

The audience applauds. Score for Gerda Hoff!

She's tempted to quote her mother's frequent comment – 'Well, you're entitled to your opinion' – but she doesn't. Instead she says, 'And that is exactly why I wrote my book: to describe the impact of those six million lives on the subsequent generations. I wrote this book so that those of us who weren't there, those of us who were not yet born, would better understand the experience of those who were present. And,' she says, 'and prevent it from happening again. Never Again.'

'So it's all a big lie?' the old woman says.

'You show no love for Germany,' the German scholar says, clearly feeling left out of the debate.

'My novel is not about Germany. It is the story of four generations of a family struggling to claim their history and their identity.'

The panel ends, and even though the members of the audience don't hold up scorecards, she can tell that Gerda came in first, she was second, and the German a distant third.

Never again, she tells herself. Never say yes when you mean to say no.

After the panel she sits at a small table signing books and answering questions.

'Are you a gay?' an old woman whispers, in the same voice her mother would ask, *Are they Jewish?* 'I think you're a gay? My son, I think he's also a gay. He doesn't tell me, but a mother knows.'

When the line is gone, she buys a copy of her own book and gives it to Gerda Hoff as Gerda is leaving.

'I don't want it,' Gerda says.

'It's a gift. I think you might find it interesting.'

'I'm eighty-three years old. I watched my parents shot in the back. I buried my own children, and now I'm dying of cancer. I didn't live this long to be polite about a piece of dreck that you think I might "like".'

'I'm sorry,' she says.

Gerda leans toward her, 'You want to know what I like? Chocolate ice cream. That's something to live for. Your book, *a shaynem dank dir im pupik*. I lived it, I don't have to read it,' she says, and then toddles off down the hall.

She finds the War Correspondent by the elevator – waiting.

'How'd it go?' he asks.

'Eviscerated,' she says.

'I wouldn't take it so personally.' They step in, and he hits the button for the fourth floor.

'They may be senior citizens, but they're pugilists,' she says. 'They're not just taking Zumba, they're also boxing, and they know where to punch. What about you?'

She looks at him; the top two buttons of his shirt are open, dark hair spinning out from between the buttons. She has the urge to pluck a hair from his chest like it was a magical whisker.

'Apart from the heckler who called me a pussy, it was okay.'

The elevator opens on the executive floor. 'So I'll see you at the cocktails?' she says, stepping out.

'Not for me. I'm on deadline.' He pauses. 'I don't think I've seen you in years except at the book awards. Congratulations, by the way. Your book is the kind of thing I could never do,' he says as he starts down the hall.

'In what way?' she calls after him.

'Fiction,' he says, turning back toward her. 'I could never make it up. I have no imagination.'

She smiles. 'I'm not quite sure what you mean, but for now I'll take that as a compliment.'

'Drink later?'

She nods. 'In my head I keep calling you the War Correspondent. Years ago I used to call you Erike, but somehow that no longer fits.'

'You called me Erike because that's what my mother used to call me.'

'You were married. We were all impressed; it seemed very grown-up. We talked about you behind your back.'

'That's funny,' he says.

'Why?'

'I was miserable.'

'Oh,' she says.

'I thought I was so smart, had it all figured out.' He shrugs.

'And why did we hang out there, at the Cedar Bar?' she asks. 'Who did we think we were? Painters?'

'Up and coming,' he says. 'We thought we were going someplace.'

'And here we are.'

There's an awkward beat. 'So what are you going to do now? I remember that you used to ride your bike everywhere. You never went on the subway.'

'Yes,' she says. 'I used to ride my bike everywhere – until I blew out my knee.'

'Do you remember that I got you to go on the subway?'

'I do,' she says, smiling. 'It was January.'

'The seventeenth of January, 1991, the night the bombing started in Baghdad.'

She nods, surprised he remembers.

'I made you take the subway all the way uptown.'

'It was a big night,' she says.

'Yep,' he says, and then seems lost in thought. There's a silence, longer than feels comfortable. 'All right, then,' he says, and abruptly heads down the hall, leaving her to wonder – did something happen?

She goes to her room and sits to meditate. Her meditation is punctuated by thinking about him. She keeps bringing herself back to her body, to the breathing and counting, until she falls deeply asleep. She has horrible dreams and wakes up forty minutes later, sweaty and confused as if roused from general anesthesia. She has no idea where she is and is trying to process whether anything in the dream was real.

The antidote – calling her mother.

'What are you doing?' her mother asks, her tone an instant reality check.

'I just took a nap. It was awful, nightmares,' she says. 'I'm away at the conference.'

'What is this one about?'

'Genocide(S). I accepted the invitation thinking of you.'

'Why me? I wasn't killed in a genocide.'

'Because of the Holocaust, because of Pop-Pop's brothers.'

'Oh, that was very nice of you,' her mother says.

'It's not about being nice,' she says, 'it's about remembering.'

'It's good you remember,' her mother says. 'I completely forgot you were going away. When are you coming home?'

'Sunday night?'

'And when are you coming to see me?'

'Maybe next weekend.'

'Next weekend isn't good. I have theater tickets.'

'Okay, then maybe the following.'

'It would be nice if you could come sooner. Come during the week. I'm not so busy then.'

'I work during the week.'

'Is that what you call creative writing – work?'

'Yes.'

'When my friends say they love what you do, I say they're entitled to their opinion.'

'Thanks, Ma, I'm glad that I work so hard only to have it embarrass you.' She takes out her computer, puts her mother on speaker.

'Are you typing now while you're talking to me?'

'Yes.'

'I hope you're not writing down what I'm saying.'

'No, Mom, I'm looking up synagogues and texting one of the conference organizers to ask if tonight's dinner is seated.'

'I'm a private person. I don't need the world to know so much about me.'

'But, Mom, the book isn't about you.'

'That's what you say, but I know better. So when are you coming to visit me?'

'I have to go, Ma. I love you. I'll call you tomorrow.'

The agitation of talking with her mother has prompted her to get up, wash her face, unzip her suitcase, and contemplate what to wear. There's a full-length mirror mounted to the wall. She looks different than she remembers, shorter, rounder. It's happening already – the shrinking?

Lisa texts, 'Are you dead? It's unlike you not to call or write.'

What's the problem? she asks herself. Is the problem Lisa? Or is it something else?

'We talked just two hours ago. Meanwhile, I had the pink one,' she writes back. It started as a joke when they were newly a couple and has become a recurring theme. 'I sucked it. The chocolate melted in my mouth,' she texts.

'Lol, not on your hands,' Lisa writes.

She dresses for temple, simple black pants and a shirt. On her way out of the building, she passes the 'gathering'. They don't call it a cocktail party because that sounds too festive, and between those who don't drink for religious reasons, those who are in AA, and those whose blood thinners or pain medications interact badly, the 'Freedom and Unity' mocktail is doing a brisk business.

One of the organizers spots her and insists she mingle. Mingling, she searches for Otto Hauser, who has still not arrived. She's introduced to Dorit Berwin, a Brit, who rescued hundreds of children from certain death in the Sudan. Dorit personally adopted fifty-four children and would have taken more, but her biological children made a show of distancing themselves from her with a public campaign titled 'They're Kids, Not Kittens'.

She finds it odd that it is Friday night and none of the conferees at the gathering seem to notice that it's Shabbos.

Around the world it is her habit to go to temple; she's the only one in her family who practices.

'What do you mean, practices?' her mother says. 'We're Jewish, what are we practicing for? Haven't we been through enough?'

'It makes me feel I'm part of history.'

As she drives over the hills on a two-lane country road, the sun is dropping low on the horizon. There are cows making their way home across fields and self-serve farm stands with fresh eggs, tomatoes, cut flowers, and free zucchini with every purchase. The sky is a glorious and deepening blue.

It's just past sunset when she pulls in to the tiny town. The raised wooden Star of David and the mezuzah are the only outward markers on the old narrow building. She knocks three times on the heavy wooden door, like a character in an Edgar Allan Poe story. She knocks again, she waits, she knocks once more, and finally . . .

'Can I help you?' a man asks through the door.

'I'm here for Friday-night services,' she says.

'Are you sure?'

'Am I late?'

'A little.'

'Can I come in?'

'I guess so,' the man says, opening the door. 'We have to be careful. You never know who's knocking.'

The synagogue is small and lost to time. There are about thirty people between her and the rabbi.

'What is it to be a Jew?' the rabbi is demanding of the group. 'Has it changed over time? We are reminded of our forebears, who were not free, who had to say yes when they meant no. We are all transgressors, exiles; there is none among us who has not sinned. It is not about the size of one's sin or one sin being greater than another – but that we are all human and thus flawed, and only by recognizing those flaws can we come to know ourselves.'

She listens, a stranger in the rear of the room, looking at the backs of heads, contemplating. Would Lisa go to temple with her? She's never asked, because she and Lisa are forever in a push-pull needing space, room, time. Lisa says they're together so much that it's hard to know where one ends and the other begins. But she always knows where she ends – she ends before she begins. She's not what she calls a 'classic lesbian', a merger, who brings the U-Haul on a second date. She is perpetually frustrated and disappointed. She wonders, is it a Jewish thing, a relationship thing, or is it just her?

The sound of a crying baby brings her back into the moment. As the woman with the crying infant leaves, she notices that he is there, up front. She recognizes him from his hair, the nape of his neck. He is four rows up and deep into it, dipping his head at key points.

Surprised but pleased, she used to think of him as serious but thought that his success had eroded that. She imagines him now as a bit more of a wartime playboy, hanging out with people like the fearless woman journalist with the eye patch who was killed in Syria. She imagines he plays high-stakes poker and has drunken late-night sex with exotic women who speak no English.

'Those saying the Mourners' Kaddish, please stand,' the rabbi intones. He stands, prays. She can tell from the rise and fall of his shoulders that he begins to cry.

And then it is over. The Shabbos has begun, and the congregation is invited to stay for a piece of challah and a sip of wine – in tiny plastic cups like thimbles.

'I didn't know you were Jewish,' he says, tossing back the tiny cup like it was a dose of cough medicine. 'I thought you were gay.'

'Like they're related, Jew and gay? Different categories. I thought you were married.'

'Divorced, but I am living with someone.'

'So am I,' she says. 'See, I knew we had something in common. What about the deadline?'

He shrugs.

'How did you get here?'

'Taxi. Thirty dollars. Do you know that the taxis are shared? You pick up people along the way – a toothless woman and groceries, a fat man who couldn't walk any farther.'

'Do you go to temple a lot?' she asks.

'No,' he says, wiping a tear from his eye.

She pretends not to notice.

'I'm starving,' he says. 'The last thing I ate was the death tuna at lunch. Do you think there's Chinese around here? In my family that's the way we do it, temple and then hot-and-sour soup.'

She shakes her head. 'No but there's a famous ice-cream place near here, wins all the prizes at the state fair.'

The ice-cream stand is set back from the road in the middle of nowhere. They find it only because a long line of cars, trucks, minivans is pulled off and parked in the dirt.

WE MAKE OUR OWN BECAUSE WE LIKE IT THAT WAY is written in bubble-lettered Magic Marker on poster board. The long summer season has taken a toll; thundershowers and ice-cream drips have caused the letters to run. The posters look like they've had a good cry.

Enormously large people lower themselves out of their minivans and wobble toward the stand.

'What I like about these gigs is the local color,' he says, taking it in.

A few late bees hover.

'Yes,' she says. 'It can be really hard to get out of one's own circle.'

'I'll go for the medium Autumn Trio,' the War Correspondent tells the boy behind the counter.

'Small chocolate in a cup,' she says.

The War Correspondent pays.

'Chivalrous.'

'Taxi fare.'

The ice-cream scoops are like a child's fantasy of what an ice-cream cone might be, the scale both magical and upsetting.

'This is what's wrong with America,' he says, digging in.

'Entirely,' she says.

They sit at a picnic table in a grove of picnic tables.

'Was your family religious?' he asks between licks.

'No,' she says. 'Yours?'

'My grandmother and my aunts are observant, but not my father, who adamantly refuses.'

'Where were they from?'

'From a town that no longer exists.'

'Mine came in a pickle barrel,' she says. 'When I think about it, I imagine the ocean filled with floating pickle barrels all the way from Latvia to Ellis Island.'

He's like a kid eating his ice cream, happier with each lick. She reaches over and wipes drips off his chin. He smiles and keeps licking.

He has three flavors, the house special: butter pecan, maple walnut, brandied coffee.

'Taste it?'

She takes a lick, eyes closed. 'Maple,' she says.

'Try over here,' he says, turning the cone.

'Brandy,' she says. She slips a spoonful of hers into his mouth, noting that there is an immediacy to ice cream, that it travels through you, cold down the middle while the flavor stays on your tongue.

'*A shtick naches,*' he says.

'*Naches.*' She laughs. 'My grandmother used to say that when she brushed my hair. She pulled so hard that for years I thought *naches* meant "knotty hair".'

'It means "great joy".'

'*A yiddisher kop,*' she says. 'Mr Smarty Pants.'

She has another lick of his ice cream, and then there's a pause, a moment, realization.

'You okay?' he asks.

'The ice cream is so delicious and you look so happy,' she says, and then pauses. 'I'm haunted by the survivors who refuse to enjoy life because it would be disrespectful to those who were lost. They feel an obligation to continue suffering, to be the rememberer.'

She tells him about Gerda and her chocolate ice cream and then asks, 'But why are we here? Why do you and I choose to live in the pain of others?'

'It's who we are,' he says. '*In di zumerdike teg zol er zitsn shive, un in di vinterdike nekht zikh raysn af di tseyn.* On summer days he should mourn, and on winter nights he should torture himself.'

'But why?'

He shrugs. 'Because we're most comfortable when we're miserable?'

'I have to remember to tell that to my therapist on Wednesday.'

He bites his cone. 'I've never been to a therapist.'

She looks at him like he's crazy. 'You've been an eyewitness to a genocide but you've never been to a therapist?'

'Nope.' He crunches.

She can't help but laugh. 'Meshuga.'

'Now, that's funny. You're calling me crazy for not going to therapy.'

They walk back to the car. 'The only Yiddish I know is from my grandmother. She wasn't exactly an intellectual,' she says.

'*Az dos meydl ken nit tantsn zogt, zi az di klezmorim kenen nit shpiln,*' he says. 'If the girl can't dance, she says the band can't play.'

They get into the car and fasten their seat belts. 'So, Rakel, you who are so good at arranging everything. Where are the *kinder* this evening?'

She sighs. 'Ah, Erike, I wanted a weekend like when we were young and used to play hide-and-seek in the pickle barrel, before we had so much responsibility,' she says. 'So the children, I loaned them to your brother and my sister. She needed help with her children, he needed help with the harvest.' She pulls out onto the two-lane road.

'It's true,' he says. 'Our boy is a little no-goodnik who has no idea of what hard work is, and our girl is soft in the head and will have to marry well.'

'Remind me, how many *kinder* do we have?' she asks.

'Ten,' he says.

'So many,' she says, surprised. 'And I gave birth to them all?'

'Yes,' he says. 'The last three it was less like a birth and more like they just arrived in time for dinner.'

'It's true. I remember I was making soup when the eighth came along, and I was bathing the fifth when the ninth announced himself, and the tenth, she arrived at dawn while I was having the most wonderful dream.'

They are quiet; a truck passes, blasting heavy-metal music.

'You know,' she says, 'after the tenth child, I went to the doctor and said, "I've lost all sense of who I am, and everything down there feels inside out." The doctor patted me on the head and said, "When the children grow up and are married, you will know who you are again. And for the rest, I'll put in a thing."'

'A thing?'

'A pessary,' she says, and then pauses and adds in her regular voice, 'I've never used that word before, but I always wanted to.'

'Can you have sex with a pessary?' he asks.

'You haven't noticed?' she says, back in character.

'When the doctor put it in, what did he call it?'

'He called it a "thing". He said, "I'll put in this thing, and you'll feel better." And I said, "Will I be able to go?" And he said, "Yes.You will go, and everything will be beautiful again."' She continues, 'The women talk about him, about whether or not he gets excited when he sees us. He stuck his finger in Sylvie's ass.'

'We're digressing,' he says.

'We're talking dirty,' she says.

And as they drive into the town, it's as though they're coming back from where they've been, lost in time.

A t the hotel, the crowd from the conference has spilled out of the bar in heated debate. Across the street the local convention center is hosting a gun show, and some of the conferees are considering a protest. There are mixed emotions. Some are desperately urging people not to take to the streets, and others feel that they must act – to do nothing is to allow the show to go on at every level.

'How do we stop the violence? I'll tell you how, we organize a group, Nothing Left to Lose. We go in shooting and keep shooting until they realize a gun is no defense,' one of the men says.

'He lived this long to be a moron?' someone asks.

'He lost his wife recently,' another says. 'He's been very depressed.'

Another man spots the War Correspondent. 'Can I buy you a drink?' the man asks, already drunk.

B efore the War Correspondent can answer, she is leading him away, down the hall. 'You want a schnapps?' she asks.

'*Makhn a shnepsl?*'

'Minibar,' she says.

When they get to her door, he flicks her DO NOT DISTURB sign. 'Are you sure it's safe? What if something gets disturbed?'

'Like what?' There is a pause.

'If I kissed you, would you hit me?' he asks.

'Is that a question or a request? If you kiss me, would you like me to hit you?'

He doesn't say anything.

She does it, she kisses him. No one hits anyone. She puts her hands up to his face, feels the scruff of his whiskers.

She likes the way he feels. Lisa is small, her skin smooth – she's a sliver of a person, like a sliced almond.

And then the door is open. He takes a Scotch from the minibar, swallows it like medicine.

'Have you ever slept with a man?'

'Is that an offer or a question?'

He doesn't answer.

'Yes,' she says. 'Have you ever slept with a lesbian? Maybe that's the real question?'

'Who initiates? Like, is it always the same lesbian each time, or do you take turns?'

She untucks his shirt. His skin is warm, the fur on his belly is long. His body is both soft and hard, fit but not muscle-bound.

'This is not what lesbians do,' he says.

'You have no idea what lesbians do,' she says.

'Tell me,' he says.

'We give each other blow jobs.'

'What do you blow?'

'Giant dildos and chocolate cocks,' she says, pointing to the still-unopened box.

'You're exciting me,' he says.

'You've always excited me,' she says. 'It's been a long time . . .'

'How long?'

'Sometime in college,' she says.

'Is it scary?'

She laughs. 'I thought you were going to say liberating.' She unzips his pants and takes him in hand.

'I really like your . . .'

'Member?' he suggests.

'Friend?' she says. 'Seriously, it's beautiful.'

'Thanks. But are you just going to examine it, or . . . ?'

'I can't help it. I love a penis.'

He laughs. 'You are so not what I expected.'

She is teasing him with her mouth, her hands, her body.

'You're killing me,' he says.

'We are at a genocide conference.'

'It's not a joke,' he says.

'Behave,' she says. 'Would it be easier if I tied you up?'

He snorts.

'How about you just lie down and be quiet,' she says.

His body is the other, in opposition, distinction, in relation. The weight of him, the musky scent, is delicious. His mouth tastes of Scotch and ice cream.

'I bet you get laid a lot,' she says. 'Do I need to worry?'

'No,' he says.

'Is that true, or do you just not want to be distracted?'

'Do you want me to use a condom?'

'No,' she says. 'I want to feel it.'

Their sex is meaty, almost combative, every man for him/herself. When he turns her over and takes her from the back, his desire is apparent. She is humbled and overwhelmed by the power of the male body. It wants what it wants and will take it until satisfied. A penis connected to a man is entirely different from the strap-on or the rabbit wand Lisa brought with her from a previous relationship.

All of them are like artificial limbs, prosthetic antifucks, but this, she thinks, this is amazingly good.

'Is this making love?' she asks, not realizing she's speaking aloud.

'It's fucking,' he says.

'Is it okay?' he asks, suddenly self-conscious.

'Yes,' she says, not thinking about him but about how much she's enjoying herself.

And then, as they're getting close to the good part, she can't help herself and anxiety pulls her out of the moment.

'Is it true that once a guy starts, he won't stop till he comes?'

'I don't know,' he says, annoyed.

His annoyance exacerbates her anxiety. 'I think it's true,' she says.

He slows down for a moment. 'What about lesbians?' he says. 'Do lesbians stop?'

'Sometimes,' she says. 'Sometimes right in the middle they just give up and stop. It fails to escalate, or someone says something and it de-escalates.'

'Do you usually talk the whole time?'

'Yes,' she says.

'Maybe that's part of the problem.'

They finish coated in each other.

The Shabbos lay is a very good thing, a blessing.

There is quiet and then sounds from across the street. 'You want to shoot someone, shoot me,' Gerda Hoff says, standing in the street. 'You like guns so much,' Gerda says. 'You have no idea. Those don't protect anyone. You want to feel like a big boy, so shoot me.'

'She's asking for it,' a young guy from the gun show says. 'Shoot her.'

'That's not amusing, Karl,' the other guy says.

'Karl. What a name, like Karl Brandt,' Gerda says.

'Who's he?'

'Exactly,' she says. 'You have no idea who you are or where you come from. Karl Brandt was the Nazi who came up with the idea of gassing the Jews.'

The guy from the gun show is impressed, like he thinks this Karl is cool.

'He was hanged for his crimes on June second, 1948. He should have been hanged six million times.'

The Novelist is at the window – the War Correspondent behind her.

'Is Gerda okay?' she asks.

'Yes,' he says.

'This isn't going to turn into some fucked-up thing where a little old lady dies on Main Street?'

'No,' he says.

'She's going to come inside and eat chocolate ice cream?' She starts to cry. 'We cheated,' she says.

'Have you ever done it before?'

'No,' she says. 'You?'

'Yes,' he says.

'You asshole,' she says, punching him.

He laughs. 'I'm an asshole because I've done it before?'

'Yes,' she says. 'If you cheat, it should be something special, not something you just do all the time.'

'I didn't say I did it all the time. *Noch di chupeh iz shepet di charoteh.* After the wedding it's too late to have regrets.' There's a pause. 'Now you're mad at me.'

She doesn't laugh. 'I'm not mad, I'm disappointed. I should get some work done,' she says.

She can't imagine actually sleeping with him there.

'Is that what you do?' he asks.

'I'm a night owl,' she says. 'And there is no "Is this what I do?" because I don't do this!'

She looks out the window again. A small crowd has formed. The guys from the gun show have no idea what's going on, except that they're in a standoff with a bunch of senior citizens. A police car rolls up, the crowd dissipates, Gerda and her gang walk back across the street.

He gathers his things. 'See you in the morning.'

She turns – he's wearing the hotel robe. 'You're going out like that?' She sounds exactly like her mother.

'Yes,' he says.

'Someone might see you.'

'I'll tell them my shower was broken and I used yours. PS, now I've seen you naked.'

He opens the door and stands for a moment half in, half out of the room. 'Do you want to go apple picking tomorrow afternoon?'

'What?'

He makes the gesture of picking apples from trees. 'Now's the moment, this is the season, the guy who gave me a ride from the airport said there's a nice orchard near here.'

She almost starts to cry again, 'Yeah, okay, after our panels we'll go apple picking and we'll play Jew again.'

'Play Jew? Is it like a game show? "I'll take Torah for two hundred"?' he asks.

'I have no idea,' she says, closing the door.

D*o you want to go apple picking?* It's the nicest thing anyone's ever said to her.

She turns on the television and calls home, not because she wants to but because that's what she does.

'Why so late?' Lisa asks.

'I was kibitzing with someone.'

'Your voice sounds funny. Are you getting sick?'

Her voice sounds funny because she just had a dick in her mouth. 'I'm just tired,' she says. 'And you?'

'All fine,' Lisa says. 'I'm here with the cat and beating your mother at Words with Friends online.' She's super proud because she just got "jest" for thirteen, but she doesn't know I'm sitting on X and Y, and I've got big plans.'

'Nice,' she says, thinking of apple picking.

S he sleeps badly. At some point there's something cold and slithery crawling up her leg, but then she realizes it's the opposite, it's 'stuff' running down her leg. She dabs at it with her fingers, tastes it.

A t breakfast a handmade Post-it hangs over the steam trays of scrambled eggs and gray sausages that look like turds: FYI – NOT KOSHER.

There are single-serving boxes of cereal and a plate of what looks like homemade babka someone has cut into pieces.

She takes a piece of babka with her coffee. Her eyes sweep the room, looking for him and glad not to see him – as long as he's not somewhere else, avoiding her. On a wipe board someone has written, 'Otto Hauser's Accepting Responsibility has been rescheduled for 9.30 this morning in Ballroom B.'

Coffee and babka in hand, she locates Hauser, the self-described obsessive-compulsive whose guilt about civilian passivity during the war led him to relentlessly collect and catalog the personal effects of those who disappeared. He is 'the' Holocaust-ephemera specialist, the man who doesn't want to be known.

'Mr Hauser?'

He looks up. His eyes are a beautiful blue clouded by the watery milk-white of old age.

'I'm sorry to bother you . . .'

He pats the chair next to him. 'Sit.'

'I'm sure you get asked all the time, but would you tell me a bit about how you came to be the Accidental Archivist?'

He pours hot water from a pot into a teacup. 'My mother was very tidy,' he says as he dips his tea bag up and down. His English is that of a German who learned to speak by listening to radio shows. 'She wasn't an intellectual, but she knew right from wrong. She was very German, very organized. So when people were taken, she would slip into their houses and recover things, before looters, mostly soldiers, came. Slowly it became known in the Jewish community, and people would bring her things to hold for them, knowing soon would come the knock on the door. My mother was very clever, good at hiding things – she put them in boxes marked as Christmas ornaments, sewing supplies, or Papa's military uniform, and they never looked. She took them to her father's farm and buried them in the field as they harvested crops. She didn't keep a notebook, but she made a code. She kept track of everything and waited for the people to come back. Near the end of the war, quite suddenly she died. I was a young man. I carried on my mother's work so she would be proud. The war undid us all – we never recovered.'

'And did the families come back?'

He shakes his head. He begins to cry, and she finds herself surprised by his tears, as though after so many years he wouldn't cry anymore. 'No,' he says. 'And still, in the fields of my grandfather's farm, we find things – a silver teapot, a pointer for the Torah, candlesticks. For years I waited. Now I'm an old man. I never married, I have no family. I'm so old that I am actually shrinking.' He gestures at his pants, which are held up by suspenders. 'I kept everything, but I realized these things should be in circulation, not in a box somewhere, unable to breathe. I started to give them to schools, museums, synagogues, to people who needed something to hold – an object of remembrance.'

'And why did you want them to take you out of the film?'

'Because I am not a hero,' he says. 'I am just a man.' Otto stands, and he is almost elfin. 'What I have come to comprehend is that it is less about the object and more about the head.' He taps his head, the aha moment, and takes off toddling toward Ballroom B.

'So nice,' one of the women says, catching her more than an hour later, as she's leaving the room. 'You don't just come to talk, you also listen.'

'You're late,' her mother says. 'You usually call at eight thirty. When you don't call, I don't get up. I don't brush my teeth. You're what starts my day. So what happened, your alarm didn't go off?'

'I love you,' she says. 'You are what starts my day, too.' She is thinking about what Otto said about the head and the transformation of the heart and the way one moves through life.

'So,' her mother says. 'If you have me to be the woman in your life, what do you need Lisa for? She can't spell. What you need with your dyslexia is someone who can spell.'

She laughs.

'I'm not kidding.'

S he finds the War Correspondent after his panel has ended and waits while he signs copies of his book. 'Yes, we did wear vests that said PRESS so people knew who we were,' he tells a man, 'but we stopped when we became higher-value targets.' What is he like as bullets are whizzing past or when men with machetes appear in the middle of the night? What is the balance between excitement and terror?

When he's finished, they escape into the day. She hands him the keys. 'You drive.'

'Rakel, I live in New City,' he confesses. 'I am a perpetual passenger. I have no license.'

Even Lisa drives.

The orchard is ripe with families and children and bumblebees buzzing. They debate between buying a half-bushel basket and a bushel and agree that a half is only a half, and so they buy a bushel basket and head into the fields.

'Erike, how was it today in town?' she asks as they walk down the rows of the orchard, past signs that say RIPE THIS WAY.

'I got new shoes for the horse, and I saw my cousin Heschl. He has troubles that one cannot speak about.'

'His daughter?'

'No, his son.'

She shakes her head, tsk, tsk, and thinks of her therapist, clucking.

Picking apples off the trees, they search for ones that are ripe, that come to them with only a tug. They polish the apples to a shine on their shirts and bite from the same apple at the same time – the skin crisp, the flavor sweet, the texture meaty and young. A few bites and then it is discarded as they hunt for the next one. He lifts her to get the perfect one from the top of a tree and then asks her to wait while he runs to the farm stand and buys a jar of honey.

He pours the honey on the apples they eat. Honey runs down his hands; his fingers are in her mouth – it's sticky.

They celebrate early New Year. Rosh Hashanah is next week, the beginning of the Days of Awe.

'I want to have you right here in the orchard,' he says, lifting her skirt, unzipping his pants, his shirt hiding the details.

Does anyone see them pressed into a tree, his comic humping causing ripe fruit to fall on their heads?

She pushes him off, laughing, 'Erike, put that away. You're acting like you've got pickles in your *keppe*. We're in public.'

Reluctantly, he zips up. 'I'll tell you something about genocides that people don't talk about.'

She waits.

'They fucked a lot. They fucked all the time, because they needed the relief, they needed not to think for a brief moment, needed to remind themselves that they were human, and because they knew they were going to die.'

'Even when the world is not at war, we all still die,' she says, picking another apple, dropping it in the nearly empty basket. There is the sound of apple hitting apple – bruising.

'When we used to hang around together, none of the guys ever asked me out.'

Another apple dropped into the basket.

'They just wanted to get laid. They didn't want to contend with someone.'

'And that's why I'm gay,' she says, dropping in a sour green apple.

'Because you couldn't get laid?'

'It's not like I couldn't get laid. I just couldn't get laid by a peer, because the girl has to be less than equal,' she says, climbing a short ladder against the trunk of a tree. 'She has to tell you that you're wonderful and powerful and all those things, but what about her? Isn't she also wonderful and powerful, or is she just the girl you fuck? And I'm not so much talking about you – you were married to your wife, whatever her name was . . .'

'Marcy.'

'You were married to Marcy, and I was busy fucking Saul Stravinsky.'

'You were fucking Saul Stravinksy? Did any of us know? He was my hero.'

'He was everyone's hero,' she says. 'And he was an ass. The thing he liked about me was that I didn't care – I treated him worse than he treated me, and he seemed to like that. And he taught me a thing or two.'

'About sex?'

'About editing.'

'Marcy and I went to hear him read at the 92nd Street Y with Philip Roth. It was an incredible pissing contest. He and Roth clearly hated each other, which makes sense – they were practically the same person.'

'I am aware,' she says. 'I was there, giving him an encouraging blow job in the bathroom of the green room.'

He shakes his head.

'You know about the ball hairs?'

Again he shakes his head no.

'Saul's second wife wrote a memoir about their marriage, *The Door Was Always Open*. She went on about how much he loved his balls because they were so big – "Bigger than Brando's," he used to say.'

'Stop!' Erike cries abruptly. 'I can't hear any more. Some things should remain a mystery.'

'I have one of his ball hairs,' she continues. 'It's what the women who slept with him did. We'd take a hair, put it in a clear glass ball, like how people do with dandelion pods, and wear them on a chain around our neck. Hairs from the nut. Twice a year we have tea, usually eight or ten of us.'

He stares at her in disbelief.

'Google it,' she says. 'One of them rather famously wrote about it.'

'We're sitting in an apple orchard on a beautiful day, we escaped a genocide conference, and you're telling me about Saul Stravinsky's balls?' He is genuinely dismayed. 'Seriously – it was all incredible. I was humping you, eating Granny Smiths, and celebrating the coming New Year. I was about to put an Empire in your mouth, truss you up against the vines, and you start talking about Saul Stravinsky.'

'Do you think you might be overreacting?'

'No,' he says. 'No.' He sits on the ground, like a child sulking.

'Really?'

'I don't know,' he says.

'Can I change the subject? This morning I heard a guy ask you about wearing a press vest, and you said that press are high-value targets now.'

He nods.

'How close are you to things when they really get going?'

'I'm standing right there. I have a flak jacket, a helmet, a recorder, a pad and pen, and a camera, even though I take terrible pictures.'

'And if you see something bad happening or about to happen, do you do something, like say, "Hey, I think there are bad guys coming" or "Wait, there's a kid in there"?'

'I'm a journalist, not a soldier.'

'But what does that really mean?'

'As I said to the guy who called me a pussy, I'm there to observe and report, not to interfere. I am a witness.'

'You stand by and watch while people are killed?'

He says nothing.

'Is there something more you could be doing?' she asks, and immediately realizes she sounds just like her mother; she's blaming him for not doing enough.

'Even if I got in the middle of it, it wouldn't change things.'

'You sound defensive.'

'I am,' he says. 'And by the way, I do get involved. I try to bring humanity to the situation. My pockets are always full of treats for the children, Starbursts and Twizzlers, because everyone likes candy and they don't melt in the heat.'

'You're involved because you give away candy? Is that what you just said?'

He stands up and faces her, like a gorilla making himself big to intimidate. 'Yes, that's what I do. I go through war zones with Smarties in my pocket. You have no idea what you're talking about,' he says. 'Your stuff isn't even real, you just make it up.'

'Are you picking a fight?'

'You're the one picking it.'

'Clever, trying to make the pickee the picker. Just because it's fiction, that doesn't mean it's not true. What you're saying is that your observations, standing there and doing nothing while people are being killed, are more important than my spending seven years developing a layered, multigenerational narrative that spans decades, giving voice to those who aren't here to represent themselves.'

'Truth is stronger than fiction.'

She almost says, 'You're entitled to your opinion,' but catches herself. 'Truth isn't synonymous with history. The point of fiction is to create a world others can inhabit, to illuminate and tell a story that stirs empathy and compassion. And, asshole,' she adds, 'fiction helps us to comprehend the incomprehensible.'

'You have no idea what you're talking about,' he says, his voice both full and tight with emotion. 'I have seen a mine explode under a woman's feet as she's carrying her baby, watched as the woman is sheared off below the waist and the baby becomes a projectile flying through the air, a vision that in another context might be magical, but here it is magic turned to murder as the baby lands on a car, still, eyes fixed, heart stopped, a life smashed. The dying mother is asking about her baby while others are gathering the parts of her body that have been separated. A man comes with her leg, carrying it like an offering, like perhaps it might be reattached. Dark blood is staining the ground. That night the mother and baby were buried together. It's too much for the brain to process to see bodies no longer whole, parts of a person. It's a shattering of the self. I helped dig the grave,' he says. 'I have helped dig many graves. How's that for the incomprehensible? Does that help? Is that doing something?'

'You win,' she says, noticing that it's the same thing she does with Lisa. She wants the fight, and then she can't deal with it. 'You saw it happen. You wrote it. You carry it with you – full score. It's both beautiful and devastating.'

'It's not a competition,' he says.

'It is, and that's what's pathetic. A minute ago you told me that what I did somehow wasn't weighty enough, or real. Is the desire to dominate, to win, fundamental to human nature? Is man's cruelty to man a fact of life? Are we such animals? There is a rank and an order that over time inevitably leads to extinction. The big question is, what are the obligations of consciousness? Can we train ourselves to do things differently? That's why we're here, asshole.'

'You keep calling me "asshole" like you've decided that's my new name.'

'We're not real,' she says. 'The true witnesses are those who died, those who were stripped naked and gassed, those who were hacked to death by others they grew up with, young men covered in sarcoma sores, wasting away, whose parents wouldn't even come and say goodbye. We are the witnesses' witness. I come to these conferences to acknowledge them; they need each other, but they also need the rest of the world to say, "I see you."'

Silence.

'There is something wrong with me,' he says. 'I keep having to go back, again and again.'

'I'm the same,' she says.

'I go around the world, to different places, to see things that no one else should see. I need it to have an effect on me, to get through to me and wake me up.'

'And then what? What would you be if you were awake? Would you realize that you're an impostor, that you're just a man in pain, not a hero, just human? And then what would you do?'

'I have no idea,' he says. 'It's like I need to be punished. Again and again I go back.'

'Well, let's find out. You're walking home from here,' she says. She has no idea where that idea came from; it just came out of her mouth.

'Have you been taken by a dybbuk?' he asks. 'It's miles.'

She carries the almost-half-empty bushel of apples and the jar of honey to the car and drives off. She has no idea what she's done or why, has no idea about anything that's happened in the last twenty-four hours. A dybbuk indeed – would that hold up in court? She drives toward town and then five minutes later abruptly turns around and goes back, expecting to find him walking along the side of the road. He's nowhere. Feeling horrible for having left him, she drives up and down looking – nothing. She leaves telling herself he's a big boy, he's been in war zones, he can get himself home from an apple orchard.

Whatever it was, whatever it might have been – done. Over. Finis.

As she's driving, she's thinking about what they were doing, the way they were playing with each other, the freedom of their conversation as imaginary others. Her mind goes back to Otto that morning at breakfast.

'The games children play – war, cops and robbers – always good guys and bad. There is something there, something about human behavior?' He paused. 'I had a frightening thing happen to me last time I was in America. I was speaking at a university in Virginia, and I went to walk around the town. There was an antiques store. I was wondering what is an American antique, what objects do they keep. So I went in. There were old ceramic bowls, heavy wooden benches, a thick black kettle one would put over an open fire, American flags, a sign from a feed store. And near the back of the store, I see something hanging; at first I think it is a decoration, a ghost for Halloween, white hand-sewn muslin, and then I realize it is something else. The head comes to a point, like a cone . . . It is a white sheet with a pointed hood.'

A t the hotel she washes the apples in her bathroom sink. She writes a note, pausing to look up the number of the Jewish New Year: '*Fresh-Picked Happy New Year 5778.*'

She brings the apples and the jar of honey down to the bar and leaves them on the table near the juices from Be My Squeeze. Philanthropy is the opposite of misanthropy.

'Y ou see what's happened, don't you?' Otto said to her that morning over babka. 'It spreads from generation to generation. It becomes the child's task to mourn because the parents can't. They survived, but they are frozen, holding their breath for forty years, not really alive. It is the job of the children, representing the dead.'

Back in her room, she calls her mother again.

'She cheated,' her mother says.

Her heart hears before her head – tachycardia. 'Pardon?'

'Lisa cheated.'

'Mom, what are you talking about?'

Her mother starts again, louder, slower. 'Your girlfriend, L-I-S-A . . . and I, we were playing Words last night on our phones, and I think she cheated. "Xyster".'

'I have to call you back,' she says, hanging up.

A break. A moment. She can't say what she did, she doesn't know;

did she lose consciousness? Did she throw something, smash her own head against the bathroom wall? Vomit? She has no idea except that time passed.

She calls Lisa.

'You mother is mad at me because I beat her at Words,' Lisa says. There is silence.

'Hello?' Lisa says.

'My mother says you cheated,' she says, too calmly.

'Are you out of your mind? Your mother kept telling me that my words weren't real. She said that "scry" was an internet abbreviation and didn't count . . . And that tone. You're speaking to me in that tone, imperious, as though you're sure you know something.'

'Fine, then tell me I'm wrong,' she says.

'I don't need to tell you you're wrong, because you know you're wrong. And you know what, Little Miss Permanent Griever, that's what I call you in my knitting group, the Permanent Griever. You're the girl who goes to Holocaust conventions all over the world and grieves for others because she can't feel anything in her own life.'

'Are you sure you want to go there?' she says, stunned. It's not like Lisa to be mean or go off.

'You know what? I don't have to go anywhere,' Lisa says, 'because you're the one who goes. You run away, you never deal with anything, you never even play Words with your own mother. Damn you,' she says.

'This is the fight,' she says.

'Yes. Damn it,' Lisa says. 'This is the fight I thought we'd have before you left, but I guess we're having it now. I guess we're having it while you're away because it would be too hard to have it when you got back, because then we'd have to deal with things.'

'Exactly,' she says.

'Exactly what?' Lisa says.

'Exactly what you said. You're right,' she says. 'You win. Touché.'

'I'm not trying to win, I'm actually trying to talk to you – but apparently that's not possible.'

'Right again,' she says.

'Stop it,' Lisa says. 'Just stop it.'

'I'm not doing anything except saying that you're right. All the things you just said are entirely right. Now what?' Silence. 'What do you want to do?' she asks.

'I don't know,' Lisa says. 'Are we supposed to do something? I just wanted to talk. Why don't we just put a pin in it?'

'*Aroyslozn di kats fun zak*,' she says.

'I have no idea what that means,' Lisa says.

'It's Yiddish for letting the cat out of the bag.'

'I'm sorry we fought,' Lisa says.

'So the note says,' she points out. 'I have to go.'

'That's it? A thunderclap argument and you have to go?'

'I have a panel.'

'You do not. I have your schedule right here. Your last panel was this morning.'

'It's a pop-up panel on Gerda Hoff, the survivor who wrote the cancer memoir, *Living to Live*,' she says, surprising herself with her impromptu fib. 'Gerda is a remarkable woman, feisty. And she loves chocolate.'

'Bring her a thing,' Lisa says.

'Not funny.' A pause. 'And I'm sorry, too,' she says. 'I really am. Everything you said is true. I suck at talking about things. And yes, for some strange reason I am deeply attracted to the pain of others. I can't say more – except to agree with you.'

'Fine,' Lisa says. 'Do me a favor?'

'What?'

'Be nicer to your mother.'

She sits, she tries to meditate, her mind is spinning in all directions. She thinks of Otto; how was it that without knowing him she had been so deeply drawn to him, had been determined to find him, to hear his story? And without knowing her, he knew her so well. She thinks of Lisa and sees that she herself is the one who is a child. She expects Lisa to demand something of her that she needs to demand of herself. She can't wait to tell the therapist, who she imagines will be impressed or worse. The therapist might say something like, You seem pleased with this idea, but what can you tell me about what it means to you?

She hears Otto's voice from this morning: 'I recently read a book that had been translated about a family where the uncles had been sent to the camps. The children, who never knew the uncles, grew up playing prison camp the way others played house or school.

'"Dance for me," the guard says, and the little boy dances. "Tell me stories," the guard says, and the little girl tells stories. "Make me some lunch," the guard says, and the children sneak upstairs and make sandwiches and bring them back down. The guard does not share. "We are hungry, too," the children say. "No food for you." "But it is lunchtime for us, too." "Eat worms," the guard says. "Now I'm tired," the guard says. "Take care of yourselves for a little bit. And while I am sleeping, walk my dog and do my homework."'

'The Re-enactments,' she said to Otto. 'That's a scene from my book.' 'It was beautiful,' Otto said. 'But you see from the way the children handled the box that had been so carefully carried from place to place for many years and how frightened they looked when it broke open and spilled across the floor that it had become a myth. And then, when the box was broken, what did they do with the treasures that had belonged to the uncles? They put them in their game. They didn't make them precious, they brought them to life.'

She wrote it. She lived it, too, in the basement of her cousin's house.

'What you see,' Otto said, 'is that history can't be contained, cannot be kept in a box. As much as we might want to keep the past where it was, it is always present. We carry it with us, not just in our grandmother's silver but in our bodies, the cells of our hearts. And that is why I am here. I am the person with the containers who wants to tell everyone – dump it out, pour it, let it spill. This is it, *bisl lam,* this is all you get. And, I might add, even for those who believe there is another world, a place we go when we are no longer here – they're not kidding when they say you can't take it with you.'

She sits, she tries to meditate, but instead she weeps inconsolably for a very long time. She weeps until she runs out of tears, and then she sits silent and dry.

He knocks on her door, face flushed pink, dripping with sweat, shirt stained, smelling like a buffalo.

'What are you so happy about?' she asks, blotting her eyes. 'You look ecstatic.'

'At first I was furious. You left me there by the side of the road. It was like you dropped me on my head. But then the walk was amazing. I crossed a Revolutionary War battlefield with the rolling hills in the background, and for the first time I had the physical sense of what it was our ancestors fought for. When I got tired, I hitchhiked. I got a ride in the back of a pickup truck with a pair of giant, very well-trained German shepherds.'

She touches something brown on his shirt. 'What is this on you, shit?'

'I think it's chocolate. I stopped for ice cream.'

'The walk was supposed to be your punishment, and you got ice cream?'

He nods, guilty, like a small child. 'I had a vanilla-and-chocolate twist with a dip into the chocolate that hardens. They called it a Brown Cow. It was fantastic. I hadn't had one since I was a kid on Cape Cod.'

'You went to the same place we went last night – it was in the opposite direction of where I left you?' she asks, incredulous.

'No,' he says. 'A different place, The Farmer's Daughter.'

She's irritated, almost jealous; he got ice cream and rode in a pickup truck. 'Everything for you is a sublime experience.'

'What have you been doing?'

'Me?' She's tempted to tell him there was a pop-up panel with

Gerda Hoff. 'I was fighting,' she says. 'With my mother and then with Lisa.'

'Ah,' he says, nodding. 'Do you know what's happening downstairs right now?'

She shakes her head no.

'Stand-up comedy,' he says.

'Holocaust humor?'

'Actually, a black guy from South Africa, followed by an open cabaret: *Songs and Stories from Distant Lands*. Do you mind?' he asks as he opens the minibar. 'I don't feel very good. Everything hurts.'

'You walked too far. Too much sun. Tylenol or Motrin?' she asks. 'Do you have any allergies?'

'And now you're a doctor?'

'At least you didn't say nurse.'

He washes down Motrin with Scotch and pulls her toward him.

'You stink,' she says, pushing him into the bathroom, turning on the shower. He can't tell if she's really mad, and neither can she.

'Do you know that I'm named after Harry Houdini? And I think that's why I slip through so many situations,' he says from inside the shower.

'What?'

'Harry Houdini's real name was Erik Weisz. He was the son of a rabbi.'

She's giving herself a cold, hard look in the bathroom mirror. She is thinking about what they both do; they are professional witnesses, reminding others to pay attention, keeping the experience alive, hoping that the memory will prevent it from happening again. She is wondering what they're both so afraid of that it has stopped them from living their own lives. She is not paying attention to him. He splashes her with water. Her shirt quickly becomes see-through.

'You want the world to see what is private to me?'

'Yes,' he says, 'I want to see you. I want to look at you the way you looked at me yesterday.'

He is pulling at her clothes.

'Stop, you're ripping it.'

'I don't care. Tomorrow I'll go to Orchard Street and buy you new underwear.'

'I hate you,' she says. 'You ever suck cock?'

'No.'

She brings the box from Lisa into the bathroom and rips it open. Three chocolate cocks fall out: pink, milk, and dark.

'Are you going to fuck me with those? Is that what lesbians do?'

'You're going to suck it,' she says.

They both almost laugh but catch themselves.

'Do you have a safe word?' she asks.

'Like my password?'

'No, a safe word for sex play, like a way of crying uncle if you want to stop.'

'Roth1933,' he says. 'It's my password, too. Now you can take me for all I'm worth. What's yours?'

'Ovum,' she says, slipping the dark chocolate dick into his mouth.

His hands find her female form in ways that are entirely different from Lisa's. Lisa likes her arms, the cut of the biceps, her shoulders. His hands are on the curve of her hips, grabbing her ass, lifting her onto him.

They are doing things with each other and to each other that have them on the verge of hysteria – they are laughing, crying. They are outside themselves, and they are themselves, and then they are asleep.

In the morning there is a circle on his chest like a bullseye.

'You have Lyme disease.'

'It doesn't happen that fast,' he says.

'Sometimes it does.'

They kiss. The kiss is deep and filled with a thousand years of longing, a thousand years of grief. They part for breath, laughing – they both know. She bites him hard on the shoulder, her teeth catching the muscle, leaving a mark.

The conference is over. There is no goodbye, because if they said goodbye, it would mean that something had ended.

'What I've learned after being the keeper of the grief,' Otto said, 'is that letting go doesn't mean you forget, but you find freedom, the room to continue on. There is the fear of forgetting, but it doesn't happen. One learns to live with the past and allow oneself and others a future. One never forgets.'

She drives to the airport, drops off her car, and gets on the plane. She wishes the plane were a time machine, a portal to another world. She wishes it would take her somewhere else.

She is home before Lisa gets back from work.

'How was the conference?' Lisa asks.

'Good,' she says as they are making dinner. 'I met Otto Hauser.'

'Your hero,' Lisa says.

'My hero,' she says.

Are they going to talk? Are they going to break up?

Lisa says nothing more about the fight, and neither does she. She brought two chocolate cocks back with her. After dinner she offers them to Lisa. 'Which do you want?'

'I just want you,' Lisa says, patting the sofa next to her. She sits next to Lisa. The cat jumps up and gives her a big sniff and makes a couple of circles before jumping across her and curling up on Lisa's lap.

Time passes. She writes the War Correspondent into a short story. He's disguised as a Buddhist poet and she as a brain surgeon. They meet when he bumps his head. They have nothing in common except a koan.

She forgets about the chocolate cocks until she discovers them one day at the back of the fridge. She melts them down and bakes them, pink and milk chocolate, into a chocolate swirl bread – a babka of sorts.

S he thinks of Otto. 'You know who comes to my talks these days? People who are still fighting. In Israel they call ahead into Gaza and say, "You have five minutes. We are coming to bomb your neighborhood. Get out." They call it "the knock on the roof". It seems polite but strange – you tell people ahead of time that you're coming to kill them? It reveals to me we have made a habit of treating each other like this. Old habits are hard to break.'

And then he took her head between his hands and kissed her on the head. '*Shepsela*,' he said. '*Du bist sheyn.*' ∎

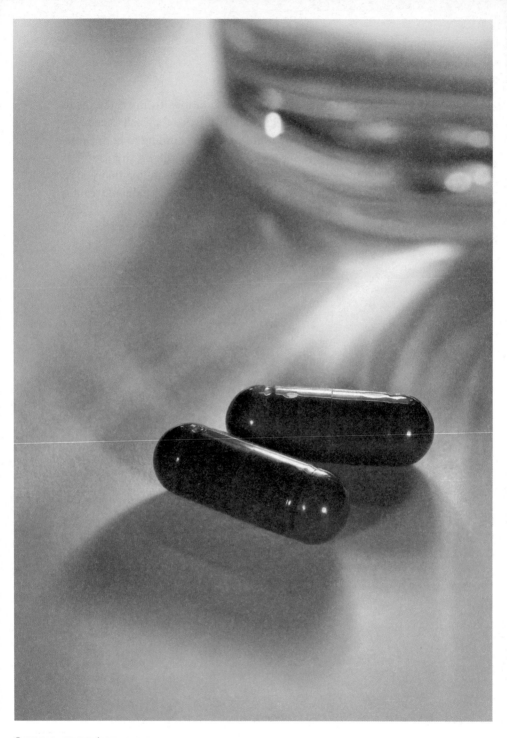

MOTHER'S DEATH

Stephen Sharp

7 August 1983

Yesterday was the most painful day of my mother's life. She told her sister, Heather, she wanted to go into a hospice. She feels there are certain things only a woman can do for her. I told Heather my mother's belief in the afterlife had caused her to give up the struggle. Mum is dopey. I got angry with father for saying how weak she had become. This morning I helped her sit up. She said 'I did not realise you were so strong.' The doctor was asked if mother could be admitted to the hospice. He said she had less than a month to live and prescribed a bottle of pink fluid. I have failed in my ambition to become a writer while my mother is alive. Perhaps I will get a part-time job as a teacher at Woodley Hill House when the academic year begins. I think mum used to read my diary. She is too feeble to reach my room now. Last night I feared after I had gone to bed father would put his head in the oven. David did not arrive home from the wedding. I feared he had been killed in a car accident. If I die there will be no one at the funeral.

8 August

Mother took less red capsules than she had been told to. The capsules are intended to avert depression. We now have to decide when she takes her tablets. I went into her room while mother was asleep and said 'I love you' twice. She opened her eyes and said 'I thought there was someone there.' I held her hand as she said she loved me. I informed her that 'we' were shouldering her out of this life. Mum said that when her body was in the graveyard it would only be a shell and she would be with God. She claimed to have seen greenery in Heaven. I cried when she said that I was the one she felt sorry for. Mother wanted an assurance from me I would help father settle down in the bungalow. I clutched her hand and said 'there is a place for you in the bungalow'. Dr Monger gives her a month. I told her not to be in a hurry to reach Heaven and that God might spare her. I almost cried while watching Bryan Ferry sing 'Jealous Guy'. I applied the line 'I didn't mean to hurt you' to myself and mum. As I lay in bed I asked God to kill me in her place. Dreamed I was in an underground train. Father, David and I decided not to send mum to a Sue Ryder home. I washed out her commode with Dettol. Helped mum put on a pair of cotton pants so she would be 'decent' for Dr Morris. The doctor thought she had a week to live. He seemed to advocate euthanasia and his only concern was that mother feel no pain. Sister Green gave her a blanket bath. The sister will come twice a day from now on. Mother finds her gentle. A cancer nurse thought Dr Morris had been pessimistic and mum would last longer than a week. Mother tried to read a prayer and said she would come with dad and me to the bungalow. I almost told her not to leave me any money as this might jeopardise my entitlement to Supplementary Benefit. I said to mother 'Do not go gentle into that good night / Old age should burn and rave at close of day / Rage, rage against the dying of the light.' I have always disliked that Dylan Thomas poem.

11 August

To quote Sister Green mother is 'comatose'. When she wakes mum has a liquid painkiller. She cannot swallow morphine tablets. When she was told Elsie had come to see her mother said 'Oh no'. While she was sitting on the commode I fed her apricot puree. It was baby food. I washed out the commode with Dettol and hot water. In a neighbour's house someone was singing 'Happy Birthday'. There was loud party music. This morning I placed my hand over my mother's abdomen and imagined it sucking the cancer out of her. David held her hand and told her she would get better. Sister Green put a substance like cotton wool into mum's pants. I doubt whether my mother will ever speak to me again. The postman returned 'Things Present' from *Granta*. It was my last chance of getting published while mother was alive. I recalled worrying about her death when I was a child, but I told her it was my own end I was fearful about. She said 'You will live for donkey's years yet.'

18 August

The funeral service was held in the United Reformed Church at 2.30 p.m. Granddad said grannie was 'worse than ever'. The minister said Thomas expressed 'our doubts'. He did not say 'ashes to ashes' at the grave. My brother threw some sweet peas onto the coffin. A train passed in the cutting beside the graveyard. This told Auntie Celia that 'life' had to 'go on'. I didn't know half of the relatives who came back to the house. A dark-haired woman called Josephine urged me not to marry just yet. An old man told me I was Granddad West all over again. Great Uncle Ernie recalled knowing my mother when she came up to his knees. The guests went down the garden to look at the sweet peas. Uncle Ivan spoke of his refusal to contribute to a charity because some of the employees were paid. The church collected more than £50 for Sue Ryder, Ivan gave £10. Father smoked menthol cigarettes.

20 August

I am struggling against Gide's assertion there are too many people for an afterlife to be possible. I found a beetle while peeling the potatoes. I fear I will never see mum again. ∎

© TOM HAMMICK
Bus Station, 1987
Courtesy of Flowers Gallery, London and New York

SNOW JOB

Brian Allen Carr

I had a liberal arts degree, and it was spring, and my friend Dolores told me that elementary schools needed men. 'We are woefully deficient in elementary schools,' she said.

'Of men?' I was eating peanuts, I think. We were at McDougal's Tavern. The smell of old carpet. Soft lighting. Bald shame.

'Of positive male role models.' Dolores had the most serious eyes. Everything she said was like an explanation. 'And not just locally,' she continued. 'Even in the good places to be from. The entire American educational system.' She gestured at America and gulped her Pabst. 'It's shameful.'

The week before, Dolores had gotten drunk on my balcony and screamed down at some dude-bros with sideways ball caps and sagging cargo shorts that all men should 'Go home and jerk off to death!' They shot her some gestures and staggered across my parking lot to wherever, and Dolores hollered out, 'Jerk off to death!' one last time as they faded into the distance. She was so amazing then.

'You think you could get me a gig for next year?'

'Positive,' she told me. She touched my hair. 'We just gotta get you cleaned up some.'

Here's something bizarre: in the spring of 2008 I tucked in my shirt, cut my hair and got a job.

I don't want to bore you with all the details of how I became a prekindergarten teacher, but what you have to know is: it wasn't my first gig at Brogan Elementary. My first year, I did fifth grade. My second, third. I sort of failed my way down to it.

For all my faults – I'm disorganized, I'm spacey, my hands are too small for my body – I've got a few things really going for me:

1. I show up. Every day. And on time.

2. I don't bitch, ever.

But I'm probably not a good teacher. I couldn't explain negative numbers to the fifth-graders and I couldn't explain nouns and verbs to the third-graders, but I can set out snacks and open finger paints better than nearly anybody alive. I can take my students to gather fallen leaves in autumn and help them do crayon rubbings. I can pour flour on the floor in December and have the kids pretend it's snow. 'I'm making an angel,' they say looking up at me, doing horizontal jumping jacks on the tile, the air in the room chalky with the dust of it all.

So, yeah, the job's a joy. A bunch of creatures with twinkling eyes doing cute things because I tell them to, but there's a trade-off.

1. They are dirty as hell. But let's come back to that.

2. You should see how the parents look at me on the first day of school.

Now, what Dolores said is true. Aside from the librarian[1] and a PE aide[2], I am the only man at Brogan Elementary. This is not an anomaly. Last I checked, the percentage of male elementary school teachers in south Texas, where I live, is something like 8 per cent, and most of that 8 per cent is comprised of coaches and Teach For America hipsters who pass through casually with their New Hampshire-soft dispositions saying shit like 'legit' and 'sustainable' until they decide their calling is elsewhere and they paddle off toward more impoverished communities in a homemade canoe. Save the world, motherfuckers.

---

[1] Who I am pretty certain is extraterrestrial.

[2] Who gives me about eighty-three high-fives a day.

But because there are so few men, parents are confused by me.

It doesn't matter if they're mothers or fathers, if they have daughters or sons: the first day is an awkward passing of the baton. The parents come in with their precious little darlings and then they have to leave them with an unfamiliar grown man.

Some things just seem wrong to us.

When I told Dolores about it, she said, 'What do you expect?'

We were at McDougal's again – they give you a discount with your instructor ID – and the crowd was thin and the music set to lull. There was an old man at the end of the bar, and every so often he cleared his throat.

'Men are perverts,' said Dolores. 'Look how much porn is on the internet. It's no wonder y'all are so shitty on dates.'

'Maybe, but there's women in those videos.'

'What?'

I sipped my beer, set it down. I was on my fifth or sixth and my coaster had gone gummy, like wet papier mâché. 'In the videos there's women.'

'Slaves,' Dolores told me. 'Caught in a system that has trained them to believe the only way they can contribute is by trading their bodies for profit, or, worse, legitimate sex slaves, trapped in brothel towns. Can you imagine? One day you're just a girl who's good at braiding hair and the next you're shanghaied to some gray sex village in Eastern Europe.'

The old man cleared his throat at this, said, 'I won't watch the ones that aren't in English.' He rubbed his mouth. 'They don't talk much, but when they do, I like to understand 'em.'

Dolores was shocked. 'Am I in the fucking twilight zone?' she asked.

The older man looked over his shoulders, surveying the empty barroom.

'I don't know,' I said to Dolores. 'I get it, guys are perverts, but women are perverts too. We watch porn. But I've seen tons of videos of women being perverted in that porn. I think we're all just gross.'

'Because they have to,' said Dolores.

'I don't know,' I said. 'They seem to be enjoying themselves.'

'Yep, yep, they do,' said the old-timer.

Dolores ground her teeth. 'Oh my God,' she said. 'They're ACTING.'

I wiped some sweat off my beer. 'Shit, then they deserve awards.'

The older man nodded.

'And,' I continued, 'if they're just acting, they need to like branch out.' Cause they're usually pretty good at acting like they enjoy the sex part, but they're dog shit when it comes to pretending they're someone's mother-in-law. They should study other methods,' I suggested.

'Stanislavsky,' said the old man.

'I'm leaving,' said Dolores. She reached for her purse. 'If you two want to sit in here and gab exploitation, you'll have to do it without me.'

'Nah,' I said. 'We'll stop.'

She had most of a vodka tonic left. She looked at it, at us. 'I'm only staying to finish my drink.'

We nodded.

'You know,' I said, 'my job might not be much different than being in porn.'

Dolores and the old-timer looked at me in unison.

'I have to pretend to be having a good time. Telling them their drawings are good and stuff. I get bodily fluid all over me. Snot. Pee. Poo. Spit. It's tons of them and just one of me.'

'Gang bang,' said the old man.

'Y'all are disgusting,' said Dolores.

'What's the worst thing they do?' the old man said. 'Like when they're misbehaving?'

I thought about it. 'Oh, y'know. Bite. Pull hair.' I gazed off. 'But really, that stuff doesn't bother me. Worst thing is when the little boys pee on stuff.'

'Pee on stuff?'

'And not just in the bathroom either. They'll go through phases. It's rare, but it happens. They think it's funny. They'll pee on the toys. In the Kleenex box.'

'It's because little boys are gross,' said Dolores. 'And they never grow out of it.' She smiled falsely.

The old-timer sipped his drink. Looked up at the grime-spotted glasses which were holstered upside down in a rack overhead. 'What about the girls?' he asked.

'I mean they'll wet their pants on occasion,' I said, 'but nothing intentional.'

'No,' he said, 'what's their equivalent? You said we're all gross. What's the grossest thing they'll do?'

'Oh,' I said, and it took me a moment. 'At nap they'll dry-hump the stuffed animals.'

Dolores picked up her glass and drained it. She set it on the bar, looked at me. 'I just can't.' She put a five-dollar bill near her coaster. 'Cover whatever that doesn't. I'm off to find healthier company.' The old-timer and I watched her go.

I wasn't kidding about the porn-star bit. Well, I was sort of kidding. My job isn't really like being a porn star, or at least I don't think of it like that. But my day consists of wrangling a horde of crazed kiddos through a routine that breaks down like this:

7.45–8.30: They start to arrive. For the first few weeks, this entails some version of me demonstrating to the parents that, indeed, I am not a pedophile, which is usually accomplished best by introducing them to my assistant Graciela who, in some subliminal manner, must intimate this to them. Then, we take their backpacks, put away their lunches and wash hands. About the fifth week of school, I no longer have to prove myself.

8.30–9.30: By this time, except when the parents are really bad alcoholics, the tykes have arrived and we breakfast on foods wrapped in plastic or fruit that looks orphaned and begin our rudimentary writing lessons. Generally, this involves the alphabet. I've been teaching prekindergarten for years now. I know the alphabet like a motherfucker. I know songs – whole songs for every letter. I know the thing in English and Spanish and German and French. I know at least two ways to turn common household materials into animals that correspond to each letter, except for X[3].

I can even sing it backwards, and sometimes I think about doing dumb shit in front of law officers while driving, just so I might have to use the skill to get out of a DUI.

Z, Y, X,

W, V,

U, T, S,

R, Q, P,

O, N, M,

L, K, J, I,

H, G, F,

E, D, C,

B, A!

9.30–10.30: Story time doesn't really last an hour, but writing lessons doesn't really last an hour either. We merely have an hour allotted. Do you know how long it takes to get sixteen four- and five-year-olds to sit criss-cross applesauce on the magic carpet? Criss-cross what, you might ask? That's right, Indian style is no more. Also, they're allowed to use their left hands now. And, it takes about eight minutes. Just to get them to sit. Then five to get them to pipe down, because they have the same questions every day.

'Is this carpet really magic?'

'It is.'

'How?'

'Metaphorically,' I'll say.

'What's today's story about?'

'A little boy who gets very sick and a stuffed bunny rabbit.'

---

[3] I loathe the letter X.

'I love stuffed bunny rabbits,' one of the girls says.

'Hopefully not too much.'

'Is the story happy or sad?'

'Only one way to find out.'

And I start reading.

10.30–11.30: Gym! Someone else handles this part. I get to go to the teachers' lounge. My first year of pre-K, Dolores had conference with me. We'd sit and gab about whatever, other teachers coming and going, making coffee or snagging their tuna sandwiches from the faculty refrigerator.

'Who teaches boys about women?' Dolores asked me once.

'Um . . .'

'Other men,' she said. 'Usually older ones who've never had healthy relationships.'

'If you knew the answer . . .'

'Don't you find that troublesome?'

'I might have learned about women from the internet.'

'My students,' Dolores told me, 'the boy ones. If they like a girl, they treat her like shit.'

'That's how they treat the boys they like too. Think about how much they wrestle.' I'd seen her fourth-grader boys leaping upon each other in the hall. Grasping each other in headlocks and half nelsons.

'I went on a date last week with a guy who tried to order for me. He tried to order for me. Food.'

Some other teacher was pouring coffee. She might have been eighty years old. 'Did he open your car door for you?' she asked. 'Regular doors don't bother me, but when they open car doors, I just get nauseous.'

'I can't remember,' said Dolores.

'Why do you even go on dates?' I asked. 'You never have a good time.'

'Because I want children.'

'Oh, honey,' said the eighty-year-old. 'You won't once you have them.'

'I want children so I can help to change the world,' Dolores said. 'I want sons. I want to mold them. You can't mold the students. I used to think you could. I think it's because they spend too much time with their parents. They come back from the weekend completely regressed.'

11.30–12.30: Lunch is odd because many of the students have dietary restrictions, and even though we give all the parents a list of things the kids aren't allowed to bring for lunch, they take no notice. Tea Party parents are the worst. You tell them at the beginning of the year about nut allergies and they say, 'Excuse me?'

'Yeah,' you tell them. 'See, one of the students,' you aren't allowed to say which one, but by the third week, somehow, everybody knows, 'is deathly allergic to nuts and we can't have them in the room, or, y'know, they might die.'

Then they mumble stuff about tax dollars, and occasionally send peanut butter sandwiches.

12.30–1.30: Music or Art! Again, this one's not on me. On good days, I'll sit in my classroom and stare at the linoleum. On bad days, I call parents and tell them what their child has done.

1.30–2.30: Math is basically code for numbers and shapes. We learn to count. We learn how some things are bigger than other things. We learn about opposites.

'The opposite of poo-poo is pee-pee,' one of the little boys will holler, and the rest of the class will erupt into forced laughter like an infomercial audience.

'Not exactly,' I'll say. 'Opposites are like hot and cold. Big and small. Inside and outside.'

'Teacher,' they'll say. 'Then what's the opposite of poo-poo?'

Sometimes, the kids will ask a question that makes your whole sense of reality unravel. Is there really an opposite of everything? Because there is no opposite of poo-poo.

2.30–3.30: The kids are supposed to leave at 3.30 on the nose, and the last hour of my day is devoted to snack and relaxing, maybe some kind of craft. This is the time we use for fake snow. This is the time we make Mother's Day cards and plant trees for Arbor Day.

This is the best part of my day, for a few reasons.

1. It's the end.

2. The kids are happy that their parents show up.

3. They're so sweet and warm when they're leaving. Walking down the hall. Singing the alphabet backwards. Waving goodbye at me. Walking their waddles.

In my third year of teaching pre-K, Dolores started dating a geologist.

'Like, really? A geologist?' I said. 'That's an actual thing? A real profession?'

'Of course it is. Why else would people study it?' There was so much fuck-you in the tone of her voice.

'You can study poetry,' I said. 'Poetry's not a job.'

She closed her eyes. 'You can be a professional poet.'

'Name one.'

She looked away. Out a window. She seemed focused on her breathing. She whispered, 'He's a geologist.'

'Fine,' I said. 'I'm happy for you.'

'Good,' she said. 'I'm happy for me too.'

I looked out the window as well, but I couldn't see anything remarkable.

'Did you tell Smashley?'

Smashley was a friend of ours who wouldn't talk to me anymore because before I got my teaching job, I'd day-drink a lot, and I was always texting, asking her to send me pictures of her feet. And then she did and felt weird about it, or maybe I was weird toward her afterward.

'Yes, I told Ashley,' said Dolores.

'What'd she say?'

'What you'd expect her to say.'

Once, when I was walking with Smashley on a grimy beach on North Padre Island, a guy in Oakley sunglasses came up, said, 'Where you going, sweetheart?' She smiled at him and grabbed her tummy. 'To take a mean shit.'

I thought about geologists. Tried to conceive of what they did. I thought about Smashley. How her brain functioned. 'She asked if he drilled you good,' I said.

Dolores had so much hate in her face then. 'I'm surrounded by children.'

'Am I right?'

'At work, children. My friends, children.'

'Did she say that?'

Dolores clenched her fists. 'Of course she said that, you fucking creep.'

There was a kind of new rage in her words. 'Wait, did she tell you about the feet thing?'

And Dolores said, 'I've always known about the feet thing.'

At the end of that semester, we had a party for Dolores in the library. Vanilla ice cream. Chocolate cake. Dolores wasn't going to be a teacher anymore.

'I'm not quitting forever,' she said. 'I'm taking the summer to plan the wedding and then next year I'm going to apply for grad school. I haven't completely decided what I'll study, but I'm supremely intrigued by the matrix of oppression.'

None of us knew what the hell she was talking about. I don't think I'd ever seen her more happy.

Sometimes at work I'll have an existential crisis. Am I teaching the students to think, or am I only just giving them memories?

I love coloring with them because it helps me make sense of it all. I give them a box of crayons. I give them a sheet of white paper and on that white paper is some line drawing to be hued. Their job is to select colors and fill blank space. My job is to give them blank space to fill. You know, if they did a good enough job in the coloring, even if the lines disappeared entirely, through magic or erasure, the form would hold. You'd still recognize the composition. My favorite kids are the ones who suck at coloring. They take the crayons and go all over the place. With them, if you removed the lines, the page would be a disaster of pigments. I like to think the ones who are worst at coloring will remember me the longest.

I barely know Dolores anymore. I got drunk at her wedding and the bridesmaids wore open-toed sandals, but that's not why.

When her son, Connor, was two years old I went to her house to pick her up and take her for drinks. Her husband was going to 'babysit'. That's what she told me. But how do you babysit your own kid?

Before we left, her husband, Ronny, said, 'You know, I don't just let any man take my lady out on a date.' I didn't know how I was supposed to feel about that.

Dolores and I went to McDougal's for old times' sake, and I asked her, 'Y'all gonna have Connor come to Brogan in a few years?' They lived in district, and Dolores was still writing her thesis and really I was just making small talk, waiting for my drink to come.

'Ha,' Dolores said. 'Ha,' she said again.

The bartender served us and we sat there and drank some and Dolores asked, 'How long do you think you'll stay doing that?'

'Teaching?'

'Ronny thinks it's funny you teach pre-K. He calls you pre-K. Like, when you text. He says, "Is that pre-K?"' She sipped her beer. 'Do you ever worry about what other men think of your job? I feel like men judge other men by their jobs. How'd you even get into it?'

'Teaching?' I said, and it occurred to me I'd been saying my job as a question.

'Yeah.'

I studied her face. She really couldn't remember. I looked away. Up at the dirty glasses, pretending to ponder. 'I think I just wanted summers off.'

I lied. It was easier that way.

This past December I was at the grocery store buying Gold Medal Flour and some eight-year-old I'd had as a student years back came up and said, 'Is that for snow?'

He pointed at the flour. I nodded and asked if he'd seen real snow yet.

'When would I ever get to see real snow?' he said, and then the next day, when it was snowing in my classroom, when the kids were lying in the mounds of it, making angels, tossing piles, I asked them all, 'Who's seen real snow?' And none of them raised their hands.

'Then this is real snow,' I said to them, and I threw a handful of it in the air and it burst open, the handful of it, a fit of fine white powder in every direction, a colorless cloud. 'This is snow,' I said. 'And if they say it's not, they're lying. And if they're lying, you don't need them. It's snowing.' I yelped a bit so they knew I meant business. I grabbed another handful from the bag. I threw it as high as I could. The children started hollering with joy. 'That's right,' I hollered with them. 'This is snow.' ∎

Nathaniel Mackey

Song of the Andoumboulou: 212

—brother b's roman sojourn—

Brother B gathered his locks, bound
   them with a tie at the back of his head.
The ponytail made his head a horse's
                ass
he proclaimed. He'd gone on a trip
and just gotten back. The place he'd
   been he called Rum. . . Next we knew
               he
said he came out of a Capuchin crypt,
   Brother Bone of late, a bite of sound's im-
position on the air. A bite of sound's
              phi-
  losophic insistence, he said. A philo-
sophic bone recital, he said, bent on
  giving one pause. A philharmonic non-
sonance, he said, gave him pause. . . The
              pony-
tail, he repeated, made his head a horse's
  ass. Don't say that, we begged, hit by
wisdom's idiocy, the wisdom of the idiots
             his.
  We'd begun to be won over, a demonic
or a divine cartoon we were in, so quick
  it made our heads twist off. A two-headed
            eagle
  had us hoodoo'd, he said, a bite of sound
on the air Nub's ancestry, Nub's predecessor

address. . . Once again, he said, the call was
                                                    to
love our captors, love them though we did
and got nothing, offer up another cheek. He
was talking out of his head but we heard him,
                                                    his
head a horse's ass but what he said stayed
with us, what he said sort of tell-my-horse.
Romulus choked Uncle Remus, he said, what
                                                    he
meant by which was worldly Rum, he went
on to explain, the lesson of ruin all over. By
that he meant to say, he went on to explain,
went on to ask, monument packed on monument
                                                    mean-
ing what. Quick blood and bone come to naught,
he went on to say, was what he meant, Rum's
feted mortality eternal. . . Mrs Fret said had no business there in the first place, picked her own bone,
                                                    phi-
losophic herself. Brother B paid her no mind. Being back made it feel like a dream, he said, a
dream he not so much dreamt as he was dreamt
                                                    by,
the dream, he raised his voice insisting, dreamt
him. A glad sadness came over us hearing him,
sound spilled out of our book. What he said we
                                                    saw,
copacetic witnesses, arms and legs rickety
sticks with a leak of spirit, this or that bodily precinct, he said, owned by a Mr Hot Pot. . . An
old song was on the box, the box's ubiquity all we
                                                    had,

the box more book than box. So it came to be
   Mrs Vex held her tongue, the music's wounded
voice, infectious, invaded hers, his and her spit's
   benediction, tongue's touch of tongue immaculate
                                    still.
   All it was was that Rum still stood, ruin's eternity,
all it was was that ruin stood still. . . Brother B was
   back, it seemed he never left, he said, his wandering
                                    eye
   the music's way-
ward kin

   (chorus)

It was song number four times fifty-seven
   but no one was counting. Brother B spoke of
there being more days in Rum than he could
                            say,
   more the more he remembered but more
than he could remember, a stone cabin perched
   on a stilt where the wind blew thru, Mr Hot
                            Pot's
   calipers made in heaven. . . He dreamt he lay
on the floor looking up Mrs Vex's dress, her
   'had no business there in the first place' pure
seduction, all of it amid stone unthinkably old.
                            What
   to say, what to say, we yelled out, an insurgent
     sneeze kept at bay inside our noses, twin pinch-
     es of next-level snuff up each of our nostrils, our
                             copa-
   cetic witness in-
tact

Rum, Brother B said, turned his head, his
   head a horse's ass after the fact. A horse's
   ass after his own heart, he said, mule as
                      much
   as horse, he said. Rum fell away from
  the tips of his toes, brick-brown expanse at
  the foot of the hill his cabin sat hoisted
on. A bamboo stilt, he said, beginning to be
                    out
  of breath, a board or a bamboo stilt stone's
  rescue, stone's mortality rehearsed. . . It
was idiot wisdom. We wanted away from it.
                    We
  wanted in, we wanted out, a conflicted choir,
   copacetic witness's relay. Brother B's way of
saying Rome made it Antillean, a move he invited us in with and we followed, heads ridden
                  hard
as his. Rum was on the ground but of the air, he
  said, bamboo bent by the storm that blew thru.
  He took refuge in the Capuchin basement, he
                said.
  We tilted our heads, high-pitched, a birdheaded breed of horse. . . It was tell-my-horse talk
  we took it. Brother B wasn't really there. Rum
said it as well as Rome, he was right. Rome wasn't
               real-
ly there. Rome undone the day he got there, he said,
  Rum run come in a day. Ruin's weaponized we,
he said, seed of empire, a dead horse left in his bed,
               he
  said, neigh not letting
go

(chorus)

Rum plied fact, feeling, the smell of whose
rooms an obtuse heaven. He stood ingesting
the bones' memo, gratuitous memo. Bone
                                re-
cognizes bone, he said. Ruin, he said, was
   Rum's middle name, trigger, tripwire, finger, its own whatever came after, all that
                            came
   after. . . All the he-said, we'd have said, a
kind of tell-my-horse, horse's-ass-headed as
   he was, birdheaded as were we, a miracle
                         of
the fishes with nary a fish in sight. We'd've
   said horse's-ass-headed, we'd've said nary,
   buoyed by the feel of each on our tongues,
                         copa-
cetic witness run
come

Brother B had us imagining a stone cot-
   tage atop a bamboo stilt, the monks' gratuitous reminder everlasting ruin, everlast-
lasting Rum. . . Meanwhile back in Nub we
                       were
   no longer athwart our skin, hot anger
   blown down our necks no matter, hot anger
   white hot, white anger, white complaint,
                     comb-
   over's would-be
Rum

PALMYRA

Charles Glass

Photography by Don McCullin

'If you ask the stars to choose a place instead of the sky
They will say Palmyra.'
—Yaseen al-Farjani

The young man betrayed no emotion as he told the story: 'They asked him to kneel. He refused. He said, "If you are going to kill me, it will be while I am standing. I will die like the date palms, upright." Because he refused to kneel, they hit him behind the knees.' The man's legs collapsed, and he fell. A sword swept through his neck, severing his head.

The young man, Tarek Assa'ad, hesitated. This was not a distant memory, and the murdered man was no stranger. It was his father, Khaled Assa'ad. The 81-year-old archaeologist died on 18 August 2015 within sight of the house where he was born on 1 January 1934. The Islamic State in Iraq and Syria (ISIS), then at the summit of its conquests, decapitated him with the same destructive fury that characterised its demolition of the Hellenic and Roman treasures that Khaled Assa'ad had dedicated his life to protecting. In the burning summer of 2015, the guardian and his city, called Palmyra for its stately palm trees, were dying together.

Tarek resumed his account, going back in time to his father's childhood playing amid Palmyra's classical temples, marketplace and sunlit theatre in the waning days of French rule over Syria. 'He was so much in love with these artefacts,' Tarek said. 'When you wake up every day and see the Temple of Bel, you have to fall in love, don't you?' The temple dedicated to the Mesopotamian god Bel, or Baal, was Palmyra's most distinctive structure. Its sacred enclosure, surrounded by porticos and columns, has fascinated scholars and travellers since its completion in AD 32. It intrigued no one more than the elder Assa'ad. He taught himself the Palmyrene dialect of Aramaic, the region's lingua franca during the Roman era, in order to understand Palmyra's elaborate inscriptions and the people who etched them in stone. After taking a degree in history from the University of Damascus, he stayed in the Syrian capital during its turbulent years of multiple military *coups d'état* to work for the Directorate-General of Antiquities and Museums (DGAM). In 1963, DGAM sent him back to Palmyra to oversee excavations and curate the new museum that had opened beside the ruins.

The energetic director uncovered hidden tombs, located the marble fort of the Emperor Diocletian's garrison, dug up hundreds of coins that had lain undiscovered for nearly two thousand years and found memorials to ancient Palmyra's notable citizens. His discoveries and publications filled gaps in the elusive history of Palmyra's rise from desert oasis a thousand years before Christ to thriving centre of world trade between Rome and India in the early Christian era. Thanks in part to his efforts, UNESCO declared Palmyra a World Heritage Site in 1980. It was no coincidence that Khaled Assa'ad named his first daughter for Palmyra's fabled queen, Zenobia, who is forever associated with the city that she led to its greatest triumphs in the third century after Christ. He retired in 2003, when his oldest son among eleven children, Walid, succeeded him as antiquities director. Retirement did not prevent him from persevering with his digging, researching, writing and educating visitors about his beloved ruins.

In May 2015, more than four years into Syria's civil war, everyone knew that ISIS militants were headed to Palmyra. They had just invaded Raqqa on the Euphrates River about 130 miles to the north and declared it capital of their new caliphate. With the Syrian Army preoccupied to the west in the more populous provinces of Idlib and Aleppo, nothing but desert and a few undefended villages stood between Raqqa and the 'pearl of the desert', Palmyra. Although strategically insignificant, it symbolised everything that the religious fanatics detested: Syria's pre-Islamic history, beautiful artworks celebrating pagan gods and ancient funerary monuments. Palmyra as repository of Syria's many cultures was to them anathema. Riding American armoured vehicles captured from the demoralised Iraqi Army, ISIS advanced south in mid-May. Its militants, led by suicide bombers in exploding trucks, opened the way through army checkpoints. Within a week, they had seized Palmyra.

By the time Dr Maamoun Abdul Karim, DGAM's director-general from 2012 until last September, learned of ISIS's intentions, it was too late to save Palmyra. The zealots had already demolished other historic sites, including Nineveh and Nimrud, in Syria and Iraq. Palmyra's Doric columns and temples were too large to move, but Dr Abdul Karim ordered the transfer of as many valuables as a small fleet of trucks could carry from Palmyra to Damascus. 'Three hours before the occupation by Da'esh,' he said, using ISIS's Arabic acronym, 'the Syrian official police in Palmyra sent twenty policemen to support my colleagues to move the artefacts. We decided to do it in the middle of the night.' While the battle for Palmyra raged between ISIS and a rearguard of Syrian troops, museum staff and twenty police commandos loaded 400 statues, along with hundreds of glass jars, ceramics and medals, onto hastily assembled trucks outside the Palmyra Museum. They worked throughout the night of 20 May. At dawn, the trucks moved out. ISIS rolled in ten minutes later.

Dr Abdul Karim told me the story in a cafe near Damascus University, where he taught archaeology before, during and after his retirement from DGAM last September. An archetypal Syrian gentleman of a bygone age, he smoked a water pipe and drank Turkish coffee. All that was missing was a red tarbush. Although aged fifty, he said, 'After the last five years, I feel more than seventy. I've had no sleep for five years.' The Syrian war saw him struggle to save antiquities all over Syria from jihadist vandals, who defaced what they called 'idols', and criminal looters, who sold their country's heritage for huge profits overseas. His efforts earned him prizes from archaeological institutes in Italy, China, Algeria and elsewhere, but at home his university would not even grant him a sabbatical to rest from his hard labours.

Dr Abdul Karim's passion for the country's past had its roots in his background, which, while not Arab, is pure Syrian in its fascinating variety. 'My father was Armenian, Bidros Krikor Eskidjian,' he said. 'In 1915, he was eight years old. His mother and father were killed.' That was at the height of Turkey's genocide of Armenians during the First World War, when thousands of Armenian orphans were roaming the Syrian countryside unaccompanied. 'He was saved by the Abdul Karim family. They are Kurdish.' His father adopted his Kurdish benefactors' name and religion, Sunni Islam. 'My mother is Syriac,' he added. Her Syriac Orthodox Christian community, like the Armenians, had suffered massacres by Turks in the early twentieth century and more recent assaults by ISIS, including kidnappings and a suicide bombing attempt to kill the Syriac patriarch in Syria on the 101st anniversary of the Ottomans' campaign against them. He summed up without a trace of self-pity, 'I am from three genocides: Armenian, Kurdish and Syriac.'

Like Assa'ad, Dr Abdul Karim studied at Damascus University, but he went to France for his archaeology PhD. The Syrian civil war was entering its second year in 2012 when he became director-general. Responsibility for all of Syria's archaeological museums and locales, six of which were UNESCO World Heritage Sites, was placed in his hands. His greatest support came from private citizens in both rebel and government areas, who hid antiquities from looters and jihadis before delivering them to DGAM. This was a grass-roots movement of Syrians – Arabs, Kurds, Armenians, Muslims, Druze, Ismailis, Alawis and Christians – to preserve their shared patrimony. 'In Aleppo,' he said, '24,000 objects were moved to Damascus in one night.' When ISIS was massing in April 2014 to assault the riverside city of Deir ez-Zor, Dr Abdul Karim's volunteers packed up 30,000 pieces and shipped them to Damascus. The basement of the National Museum of Damascus overflowed with Syria's most valuable historical relics.

Meanwhile, the trade in stolen artefacts from Palmyra and elsewhere was flourishing. Stolen statues, manuscripts, jewellery and ceramics turned up in Europe via Turkey, Lebanon and Jordan. It was not as bad, however, as Dr Abdul Karim had feared: 'We found that more than 70 per cent of the traffic outside Syria is fake.' Many items, when their provenance was revealed, went back to Syria with the help of Interpol and other police agencies. 'It's not just our culture,' Dr Abdul Karim said. 'It is a universal heritage.'

Shortly after conquering Palmyra, on 27 May, ISIS released an eighty-seven-second video message promising to preserve the Roman ruins. That did not prevent ISIS a month later from initiating the systematic destruction of the graceful colonnades that stretched into the desert for nearly a mile along the ancient Roman road. Militants smashed the famed Lion of al-Lāt, a beautiful stone statue of a lion god protecting a gazelle that Polish archaeologist Michał Gawlikowski discovered only in 1977. Subsequent reports from Palmyra were vague about what was happening. Then, in late August, satellite photographs confirmed that ISIS had razed the site's most impressive structures, the Roman-era Temples of Baalshamin and Bel. UNSECO head Irina Bokova called ISIS's vandalism a 'war crime' and an 'intolerable crime against civilisation'. ISIS followed those outrages with the destruction of Palmyra's distinctive funeral towers that had stood for centuries at the fringe of the old city. If the jihadists stayed much longer, archaeologists feared, nothing would remain.

History may not be, as Henry Ford called it, 'bunk', but it can be contentious and usually serves rival masters. Myth surrounds the ISIS occupation of Palmyra from 2015 to 2017 as much as it clouds the tale of Queen Zenobia seventeen centuries ago. Zenobia inherited the Palmyrene throne from her husband, Rome's ally and vassal Odaenathus, when he was assassinated in AD 267. Zenobia, said by contemporaries to have been both beautiful and so chaste that she made love to her husband only in order to have children, claimed kinship with antiquity's other great queen, Cleopatra. Historian Yasmine Zahra wrote, 'Zenobia was a Roman to the Romans, a Pan-Hellene to the Greeks, but in fact she was a Hellenised Arab.' Zenobia came to power when the trading centre of Palmyra enjoyed its greatest revenues and the Roman Empire was suffering what historians call 'the crisis of the third century' with rebellions east and west threatening its unity. Zenobia took advantage of Roman weakness by conquering all of Syria, Egypt and part of Anatolia. When the Emperor Aurelian consolidated Rome's control of the west, he led his army against her in 272.

Some chroniclers wrote that Aurelian killed her in battle, while others, like sixth-century Byzantine historian Zosimus, claimed that the emperor carried her as war booty to Rome, gave her a house in Tivoli and let her mature from exotic beauty into respectable Roman matron. In our time, observers differ on what transpired in Palmyra when ISIS conquered the city in May 2015, withdrew under Syrian and Russian assault in March 2016, returned nine months later and fled for the final time in March 2017.

Syrian President Bashar al-Assad's defenders maintain that the United States sent ISIS into Syria, while his opponents blame him. In Palmyra, several civilians swore to me that they had seen American warplanes flying in support of ISIS. Others said the Syrian Army assisted ISIS's conquest of Palmyra.

Last October, I went to Palmyra for the first time since 1987. Syria thirty years ago was an island of peace between Iraq, then in its fifth year of war with Iran, and Lebanon, whose civil war had another three years to run. Palmyra's ruins stretched over acres of a tranquil, isolated plain. Its allure owed as much to its position as to the structures left by the ancient Palmyrenes. 'The beauty of Palmyra is its silence,' Dr Abdul Karim told me. In this, he shared the view of Sir Mark Sykes. Sykes, whose famous 1915 accord with French diplomat François Georges-Picot is not blameless in the Syrian tragedy, had written in his 1904 travelogue, *Dar-ul-Islam*, 'The real attraction of Palmyra is its solitude; the great noisy money-proud city overturned, shaken and deserted, the sand-worn colonnades, the crumbling temples, the ruined tombs, unprepossessing in themselves, have been beautified by decay, and rendered pathetic by their forlornness and silence.' Nothing had changed when I saw it more than eighty years after Sykes. Palmyra was an exquisite diadem at the eastern edge of what had been the Roman world, its grandeur enhanced rather than diminished by millennia of neglect.

Until the 1930s, semi-settled nomads had lived in mud hovels within the ruins. The French Mandate authorities moved them into Tadmor, the town that was expanding on the northern and eastern outskirts of Palmyra. The French had already built a prison there to hold (and torture) Syrians who fought for independence in the uprising of 1925. Syria's post-independence governments kept the prison. It became the scene of the bloody murder of hundreds of political prisoners by the notorious Rifaat al-Assad in reprisal for the attempted assassination of his brother, President Hafez al-Assad, in 1980. I wrote about Tadmor in *Tribes with Flags: A Journey Curtailed*:

> Few buildings in Tadmor seemed over two storeys high, but every roof had steel rods sticking out ready for a new floor to be added when a son married. The only building materials used in the last twenty-five years were those which cursed the whole Levant: grey breezeblocks and concrete of numbing uniformity. The old, simple houses of mud or stone were beautiful by comparison, but few remained.

Tadmor town then was as squalid as Palmyra's ruins were majestic, but it was intact, and its people were hospitable. The ISIS occupations and the government's battles to retake it have ravaged it.

When Don McCullin and I returned to Palmyra and Tadmor, we remembered them as they were before ISIS. Don ran to the Temple of Bel, which he had photographed for his 2010 book *Southern Frontiers*. Little was left of the monument he had painstakingly recorded. The empty horizon loomed over shattered stones. 'Don't photograph the Russians,' a Ministry of Information official warned him as he climbed atop a massive hunk of limestone.

On this latest visit, I went into the town to find streets clogged with war detritus, water and sewage pipes crumbled and buildings collapsed with their innards exposed to the elements. Barely a hundred people out of an estimated pre-war population of 70,000 have returned. Among them were the al-Khateeb family, who had reopened their 'supermarket', a small room on the ground floor of the building where they lived. Twenty-six-year-old Ghaith al-Khateeb was running the shop for his father, Issa. The young man offered me coffee and talked about life in Tadmor while Russian soldiers loitered outside.

He shed light on one point of contention: whether the army had aided civilians to evacuate or abandoned them in its hasty retreat in May 2015. He said, 'The army facilitated the flow of the civilians. Some stayed, about 300 people.' He had fled with his father, mother, two brothers and two sisters to relatives in Homs. They came back after the Syrian Army expelled ISIS in March 2016 and reopened the shop.

The Russians celebrated victory in Palmyra with a concert in the ancient theatre. On 5 May, Valery Gergiev conducted the Mariinsky Theatre Orchestra in performances of Prokofiev and Bach to an audience of Russian and Syrian military personnel. 'We protest against barbarians who destroyed wonderful monuments of world culture,' Gergiev declared. 'We protest against the execution of people here on this great stage.' Russian President Vladimir Putin appeared on a video screen to praise his troops for their 'fight against terrorism without sparing their own lives'. The ceremony proved both premature and vainglorious. The following December, ISIS returned.

ISIS's second conquest of Palmyra astonished everyone, and fed the belief in a Syrian government conspiracy to assist ISIS. Russian and American satellites should have spotted ISIS fighters speeding across the barren landscape and given US-backed rebels or the Syrian Army time to defend the city. Colonel Sami Ibrahim of Syria's Military Media Department, sitting in a shaded bunker beside the T4 oil pumping station about forty miles west of Palmyra, said it did not happen that way. 'The second time, they made use of some of the enclaves that were not liberated,' he said. He showed me photographs of tunnels that the ISIS fighters dug into rock outside Palmyra, when they fled from the city in March 2016. The deep tunnels were covered in gravel as camouflage from aerial reconnaissance. ISIS did not come all the way across the desert from Raqqa, he insisted, but infiltrated from positions nearby. That December, the Syrian Army, with Russian air cover, was concentrating on the expulsion of rebels from eastern Aleppo. Aleppo became the decisive battle of the war, initiating the steady return of more and more territory to government control and undermining international support for the rebels.

On its return, ISIS resumed the destruction of ancient monuments and the execution of those it labelled *kafirs*, non-believers, until the army drove them out again in March 2017. The Khateeb family had again taken refuge in Homs and returned to Palmyra with the Syrian Army to reopen their shop. Khateeb led me from the modest grocery to a souvenir emporium below selling trinkets, small carpets, handmade mother-of-pearl boxes and plaster replicas of the Roman temples. 'At first, we opened a supermarket,' he explained. 'We saw that souvenirs were in demand, so we concentrated on such items.' The souvenir buyers were the Russian troops who patrolled Tadmor's streets on foot, lodged in dispersed barracks, including one inside the Roman ruins, and appeared to act as a guarantee against a third ISIS invasion. One Russian soldier used his few words of Arabic to negotiate the price of postcards and mementos to send home. Another soldier examined several items under the glass counter without buying any, much to Khateeb's amusement.

Khateeb pointed to a huge opening gouged in the wall. He explained, 'They put holes in the walls and linked all the basements.' His basement had been an ISIS field hospital. He had cleaned it up to install the shop. 'Business is okay,' he said. The only customers were Russian and Syrian soldiers. Most of the inhabitants of Tadmor were waiting for the restoration of electricity and running water before returning. Khateeb kept the lights on with a small generator that vibrated outside. 'I'm happy and unhappy at the same time,' he said. 'All my friends have left. Will they return? *Insha'allah.*'

A few streets away, Mohammed Khalid Allawi was grilling meat on a wood fire in the street in front of a shabby restaurant that was little more than a concrete box with a few tables. Beside him, his wife, Daline, and Aunt Fouda were washing and chopping vegetables. 'The army helped us get out,' he said, 'or we would have been executed.' Although he was a practising Muslim and both women wore scarves over their hair, he said of ISIS, 'They think of me as a *kafir*. They believe they are the custodians of religion. What kind of religion do they believe in?' He said that Christians had lived among Muslims in Tadmor, until ISIS drove them out. No one knew whether they would return.

Turning meat on the fire, Allawi continued, 'This is our home. This is my work. I hope all the residents will be back. Thank God, it's safe all around. We fled twice.' Did he think he would flee again? 'No. It's finished. It's only a matter of one month or two and they will be driven out of all Syria.' He directed me to a Christian church nearby. ISIS had burned it to a husk. The only signs of worship were the torn pages of charred hymnals.

Everyone in Tadmor had a story, none of them happy. A 51-year-old man slouched in a chair inside his tiny sandwich shop was staring at a vacant lot opposite. He invited me to sit and gave me Turkish coffee in a plastic cup. He introduced himself as Mohammed Saleh

93

Ali Mahmoud. 'I used to be a wealthy man in Tadmor,' he said. 'Take a look. See what I'm left with.' It wasn't much. A few shelves of biscuits and tinned milk, loaves of Arabic bread in plastic wrap, a desk. Before ISIS occupied Tadmor the first time, Mohammed ran a building firm and a lucrative business leasing heavy construction equipment. His main customer was the Syrian Army, whose engineers were involved in various building projects in the region. 'When Da'esh came, I left after two days,' he recalled. 'My son Adnan stayed.' Adnan was twenty-six and unmarried. He worked for his father. His father advised him to leave, but he stayed to protect the company assets. ISIS looted the family's house and seized the heavy equipment. Mohammed said, 'They said I'm a *kafir* and distributed my property to people they knew, to Da'esh people.' Adnan hid in a friend's house, while ISIS hunted down everyone it suspected had connections to the Syrian regime. 'Someone told them he was hiding there,' the father said. 'One of our relatives, who had come to Homs, phoned me and told me about it.'

ISIS put scores of people on trial, including Adnan. Mohammed told me that they sentenced him to death and beheaded him. Later in our conversation he said they shot him. When ISIS retreated the second time, they took some of his machines with them and detonated the rest. 'I lost everything,' he said, 'but I wish they had taken everything and left my son.' Unable to find Adnan's body, the family could not hold a funeral or bury him. ISIS had anyway despoiled graves of those whose bodies were found. 'They even destroyed the tombs,' Mohammed said, referring to the empty land in front of us, formerly a burial ground the size of a football field. Its elaborate tombstones were now pummelled to dust. 'According to the Wahhabis,' Mohammed said, referring to ISIS's Saudi Wahhabi ideology, 'tombs should not be more than six inches above ground.' I walked across the street to the cemetery. The graves were no longer discernible in the rubble that was, indeed, no higher than my ankle.

*

'The destroyers came from out of the desert. Palmyra
must have been expecting them . . . These men moved
in packs – later in swarms of as many as five hundred
– and when they descended utter destruction followed.
Their targets were the temples and the attacks could be
astonishingly swift. Great stone columns that had stood
for centuries collapsed in an afternoon; statues that had
stood for half a millennium had their faces mutilated in
a moment; statues that had seen the rise of the Roman
Empire fell in a single day . . . The zealots roared with
laughter as they smashed the 'evil', 'idolatrous' statues;
the faithful jeered as they tore down temples, stripped
roofs and defaced tombs . . .'
– Catherine Nixey, *The Darkening Age*

Nixey described devastation, not by modern Muslim fanatics,
but by Christian vandals in the third century. The Christians
attacked the statue of the goddess Athena with particular ferocity,
smashing 'the back of Athena's head with a single blow so hard that
it decapitated the goddess'. They cut off her helmet and severed her
arms. Seventeen centuries passed, as monotheism, first Christian and
then Muslim, flourished. Then, in the twenty-first century, Athena
suffered another assault. 'In Palmyra,' Nixey wrote, 'the great statue
of Athena that had been carefully repaired by archaeologists, was
attacked yet again. Once again, Athena was beheaded; once again,
her arm was sheared off.' ISIS was, in its exuberant annihilation of
the past, heir to the impulse that had motivated Christian fanatics
of the earlier time.

The Palmyra I visited in 1987 and again last year had survived
wars, rebellions and massacres over centuries. Within the grounds
of the ancient city, nothing was as I recalled it from thirty years
before. The triumphal arch was gone, its plinths silhouetted against
the bare sky. The Temple of Bel had become a sea of broken stone
that archaeologists believe will take a generation to piece together.
The agora was unrecognisable. Wandering through ancient

Palmyra in 1987, I could reflect on Queen Zenobia of Palmyra, her rebellion against Emperor Aurelian and the destruction, as well as later restoration, of her city. Zenobia had inspired historians to embellish her image, Boccaccio and Chaucer to celebrate her stamina, nineteenth-century American sculptor Harriet Hosmer to immortalise her in stone and the glamorous Anita Ekberg to portray her in the dreadful sword-and-sandal movie, *Sign of the Gladiator* (1959). The latest chapter of Palmyra's history offered no nobility to portray, to immortalise or to glamorise. The only consoling fact of the modern vandalism was that it could have been worse.

When ISIS prepared to abandon the site for the second time in March 2017, it placed so many charges throughout the ancient city that Russian and Syrian sappers needed months to remove them. The miracle was that the bombs did not explode. Like Hitler's order to destroy the historic heart of Paris before the German Army retreated in 1944, the demolition failed. Either there was no time or a local commander – a latter-day General Dietrich von Choltitz – refused the order to erase so much history and beauty from the face of the earth. Palmyra, despite the depredations to its monuments and its people, survived. For now. ■

The Roman Theatre

The Great Colonnade

The Temple of Bel, cella

The Temple of Bel, inner facade of the gate

The Agora

The Great Colonnade

The Roman Theatre

The Imperial Temple

The Temple of Bel, outer walls and gate

The Temple of Bel, courtyard

The Temple of Bel, courtyard

The Monumental Arch

DEADLINE 1 OCTOBER 2018
www.mslexia.co.uk

WOMEN'S FICTION AWARDS 2018

mslexia

'the wilder will teach the wolves how to be bold again,
how to hunt and fight, how to distrust humans' FROM THE WOLF WILDER BY KATHERINE RUNDELL

With a range of categories from 100 to over 100,000 words, and prizes totalling
£12,000, there is bound to be a competition here to suit you

CHILDREN'S NOVEL, NOVELLA, SHORT STORY, FLASH FICTION
Four fiction awards - One career-changing opportunity

Supported using public funding by
ARTS COUNCIL
ENGLAND

mslexia.co.uk
0191 204 8860
postbag@mslexia.co.uk

LAKE LIKE A MIRROR

Ho Sok Fong

TRANSLATED FROM THE CHINESE BY NATASCHA BRUCE

If she'd swerved any harder, she would have crashed right into the lake. In the eerie twilight, the deer seemed to come out of nowhere, darting silently into the road. Of course she'd been startled. And for a few seconds all she'd wanted was to run – throw caution to the wind, shake off gravity, be gone.

In recent years, she'd watch students bent over their desks, pens softly scratching, and a scene from the nature channel would float into her mind. A herd of elk in long grass, nestled meekly against one another. She had no idea how they grew or reproduced but, ever since that programme, thought of them often. Their chestnut fur and affection for each other. How they were wary by nature, and never spoke – at least not that humans could hear – and liked to chew on leaves. They probably had fleas, there was no way around that; every animal does. But, then again, maybe none of this was true. Maybe it was all wrong. It wasn't based on anything, and biology had never been her strong point.

No one ever broke the rules. Hushed chatter rose from the desks, occasionally crescendoing into the crash of an ocean wave, or the clamour of a wet market. Sometimes a question would leave the class in deathly silence. Sometimes an eager voice would pipe up and shatter it.

'I don't think things are as bad as the protagonist makes out.'

'Why do you say that?'

'The narrator is so fixated on her own suffering, it's way too heavy-handed. The novel opens with, "Fear torments me, making me almost lose my mind." Right from the start, it's just one crazy woman ranting to herself.'

'But the tone is very detached. What's your basis for calling it heavy-handed?'

'I actually like the victim,' someone else chimed in. 'Maybe she enjoys the misery. Do you think it's easy to write from a victim's perspective?'

'It's an easy way to win sympathy from a reader.'

Bursts of laughter, sighs, some students nodding, others shaking their heads.

A brief debate. Whispers over the desks from those who didn't participate. She waved her hands to quiet them, pressing lightly on the air, as though conducting an orchestra.

'Do we have to rush to a conclusion? Are there clear answers, or could it be that the ending is left open to interpretation?'

She liked talking to them. Their voices filled the classroom, rising and falling like bouncing cicadas.

'But is it so difficult just to say what happened? Why does it have to be so ambiguous?' said one student.

'This is why I hate metafiction,' said another, picking up her books and hugging them to her chest as she walked out. 'It's too hard to understand.'

Even the sighs and complaints sounded like the low moan of a plucked string.

There was a telecom tower outside the classroom window. Through the slits in the blinds, it looked small and far away, like a tiny decorative sticker that kept sliding into her line of vision. When the pollution was bad, it was hardly visible, but in the evenings, driving home along the expressway, she could see it clearly in the distance, tip flashing boldly. An inland lighthouse, high above the sea of lights below, alone and cheerless in its corner of the night sky.

Our lives depend on it, she'd think to herself, every so often. Imagine that. Without it we'd be so much lonelier. But the tower itself didn't know. It sent out hundreds of thousands of messages, every single day, and it had no idea.

For a long time, she'd been careful to steer clear of trouble at work. She was thirty-five and had held her position at the university for four years, but still felt like a baby just learning to crawl. The most she ever spoke was in the classroom. And sometimes she wondered what those docile young elk took away from her classes. Another day rolled past, and what had she said? Had she been careful enough? Could someone have misinterpreted her words? Had she been true to herself? She'd been heeding these warnings since her very first day.

'They're very young. They may look like adults, but inside they're still children. In many ways, they don't yet know right from wrong, or understand the potential consequences of their actions. As their teachers, we have to be extremely careful what we say.'

This was said so seriously, she almost wanted to laugh. But no one else in the room seemed to find it amusing. Several teaching contracts had expired, and would not be renewed. This was announced at the meeting. Announced, not discussed: the committee had made its decision. Very little was said. Items were read aloud and token comments were added, as usual. It was a routine affair, during which no one would object and nothing would change.

The colleague beside her sighed softly. She heard him shift closer. 'Better not go making problems round here,' he whispered. 'Don't be like them. Sued, fired . . . didn't you start at the same time as her? Did you know her?'

She said that she wasn't sure. Maybe in passing.

At the front, the chair was still giving his earnest speech.

'We must respect others, be mindful of not interfering where we don't belong. You need to be vigilant, because your students are sensitive, and so are we. Very, very sensitive.'

She flipped through the meeting notes on her lap.

A slogan from the government's public service department was printed along the bottom of the last page: IN SERVICE TO OUR COUNTRY AND ITS PEOPLE.

Her parents had also been public servants. Her mother, a primary school teacher, and her father, a primary school headmaster. From time to time, the same slogan had appeared in their house, emblazoned on a new mug or towel or umbrella or fountain pen or folder; souvenirs from training courses her parents had attended during the school holidays. She'd never thought much of it. The umbrellas would break, the towels would get mouldy, the mugs would smash. Now, for the first time, she felt like the sentence was trapped in her chest, as hard and unyielding as a stone.

'Remember: it's your job to be more sensitive than they are.'

I am very sensitive, she thought. It was a feeling like a thorn buried in her forehead, ready to work its way out through the corner of her mouth and pop the bubbles of chat and laughter that hung in the air. She avoided it carefully, wary of snags, but still felt uncertain. Most days, she parked under a shady tree; most days, she sat there in the driver's seat, staring into space. Windows rolled down and the world around her surging like a sea. But she was inland, all was still. No waves. A light breeze blew through the car park lot, rippling the surface of the biology department's fish pond.

She had an excellent memory. She could churn out names, dates and author biographies without thinking, and would write them in long lines across the whiteboard. It intimidated people. Perhaps it was even too excellent a memory, because everything she heard stayed with her. It took a long time for her to let things go.

'We all have to learn to forget what isn't worth remembering,' said her mother.

'All I have is a pile of things I need to remember,' she replied.

She reminded her mother, who was killing a fish, that the fish was already dead; that she couldn't kill it twice.

'Don't correct me,' said her mother, slicing open the belly and scraping away the innards. When she was little, she remembered asking why fish couldn't close their eyes. Her mother had said that fish saw everything, and that was why eating them made you clever.

'In the end, aren't we all just fish on someone's chopping board?'

'Go back to your books!' snapped her mother. 'You must have better things to do. Make yourself useful!'

She went onto the balcony to keep her father company. He was smoking, looking out on the familiar view, and his face lit up at the sight of her. There was a Chinese primary school on the hill opposite, producing intermittent bursts of clarinet music. Her mother claimed to have heard sparrows that were more rousing, but today she liked it. Every so often, names were called out over the speakers. Huang Weixing, please report to the office. Or: Ye Yunxin, Ye Yunxin, where are you? And everyone in the surrounding area would hear these names and know that these people were being looked for. She imagined a teacher standing before a rank of students, yelling into a megaphone. She imagined those Chinese schoolchildren lined up as straight and orderly as soldiers. A tiny Communist Party – that's what she and her classmates at the convent used to say. She didn't know any of the Chinese kids. They were just voices floating down the hill, sometimes drowned out by the shrieks of nearby children, or the sound of the television. She didn't know why she'd been so resistant to becoming a primary school teacher; it would have been much simpler than her current job. So much more relaxed.

'If they won't behave, then teach them a lesson,' said her father, solemnly imparting his wisdom. 'Make an example of someone. Don't be soft. Don't let them think you're a pushover.'

At the dinner table, they talked about family. About her cousins, who were around her age. Which ones were doing well, which ones were wasting their lives, which ones were beyond all hope.

'She won't even see her siblings,' said her mother. 'Before it was bad, but this is a whole new level. Always fighting with her bosses, can't hold down a job.'

'People like that never get far,' said her father. 'They specialise in biting the hand that feeds them.'

She hadn't seen these relatives for a very long time. When they were mentioned, she had only the faintest impression of who they were, like fragments from an old dream. Her parents acted surprised by her forgetfulness, mystified that she couldn't recall her childhood playmates, but she'd left her Chinese primary school before finishing; her parents had been posted somewhere else and she'd had to transfer. Then they'd sent her to an all-girls convent for secondary school, and the three of them drifted apart from the rest of the family. She and her cousins had grown up to be very different people. Still, she struggled to imagine them as either these smug success stories or abject failures.

'How do you know all this,' she asked. 'Who told you?'

'People talk.'

She thought of one summer holiday when she was a child. At her grandmother's house, gathered on the shore with some of the cousins, watching her uncle plunge into the water. Into that big, deep lake. People were casting fishing nets off floating platforms, marking them out with rows of tightly bound bamboo, dividing the surface of the lake into little kingdoms. Her younger cousins said her uncle could dive and fix the nets underwater. He tied a thick rope around his waist and jumped. She went to the adults standing guard, and asked when he would come back up. They said she had to wait and see.

She crouched at the edge of the water, and a head suddenly broke the surface. Ripples erupted from the centre of the lake, radiating in big, widening circles that sank into the wet mud of the shoreline. She wasn't sure which she'd seen first: the ripples or the person.

'Your uncle has incredible stamina,' the adults said, using the English word. 'Fixing the nets is no mean feat; he has to hold his breath, keep his eyes open to find the holes, and then stitch them back together. He has to make sure he has enough air for all that time.'

The sun was so bright that afternoon it made her dizzy. She lost count of how many times her uncle came up for air. Each time he surfaced, he opened his mouth wide to the sky, as if trying to inhale the clouds.

She asked why they didn't just pull the nets in, and an older cousin told her it was too difficult, because they were big and heavy, with ropes and nails fixing them in place. Dragging them in would only tear more holes.

Talking too much was risky, and so she talked very little. She limited herself to explanations; the necessary clarifications. In the classroom with her elk was the only place she was calmer. She liked their energy and intelligence. Their naivety. She liked how respectful they were. Liked that they asked questions and paid attention to her answers. They were very similar to her, she discovered: fond of leisure, averse to pressure. She felt less conflicted when she was around them.

If you asked them who they admired, they'd say Maugham, Carver, Tolkien, Harry Potter. No one mentioned Mann, Hemingway, Faulkner or Woolf. If you asked why, they'd make faces.

'Hemingway's dialogue is all over the place and I don't understand it,' they said.

'Too many new words, too many characters. The relationships are so confusing.'

If she discounted the silent ones and painted each of those ringing questions, hypotheses, conclusions and retorts a different colour, the classroom became a vivid tapestry. She was not displeased, to have woven such a scene. Who knew whether she would have had the opportunity anywhere else. Sometimes, she imagined they were animals calling to one another in a forest, each voice coming from its own shadowy location in the trees. She tried to coax out the shyer ones. First, of course, they had to be allowed to listen quietly. But they couldn't be beautiful if they let themselves merge into the same colour as the leaves.

Sometimes, the debates were so engrossing that she forgot those initial urgings to be cautious. Forgot how she used to think of herself as the wind, working invisibly in the background, conducting other people's performances. The students had different accents when they spoke English. Indian and Chinese were the most common, Malay the least. There were only four Malays in the class, and three of them stayed as quiet as shadows. The only one who didn't was an animated boy, slight but always stylishly dressed. On hot days, he turned up in tight-fitting shirts and Capri pants, wearing shoes with pointed toes. He gesticulated exuberantly when he spoke, making the silver bell on his charm bracelet tinkle.

He was from the drama department.

'If this novel's adapted for the stage, I was born to play the part of the beautiful young Venetian.'

Whistles, cheers, boos.

He fluffed his curls. 'No one could be better suited.'

'You've got black hair!' There was a flurry of laughter. 'And you're already too old!'

She let him carry on. She doted on – was delighted to indulge – the students with obvious literary talent. She had the class read aloud from e.e. cummings' 'Spring is like a perhaps hand'.

and | without breaking anything.

They were happy, and their enthusiasm made her feel young. The boy read aloud with such rhythm, almost as though he were singing. 'I like "i like my body", ' he said. There were still ten minutes left of class, so she let him read it. She didn't think too much about it. The poem was beautiful, and she couldn't resist beautiful things.

As he read the electrifying lines, she was struck by his beauty. His eyelashes were very long, and fluttered along each sentence. If the poet were alive, she thought, he wouldn't fault him. Notes launched from the tip of his tongue and thrilled along her spine. In places, his voice went as taut as a violin string; in others, it spread wide as an opened letter. She didn't notice that students were leaving the classroom.

That was April, and April passed quickly. Wind stirred the dead leaves, making them march across the ground like an army. Every so often, she'd feel calm and steady, like a clump of firmly rooted plants, with no more need to worry about falling over. She weeded in the garden at home, and noticed soft, new shoots pushing through the earth. The cuttings she'd planted earlier in the year had quickly shrivelled, but there had been a spell of rain and they were struggling back to life. Spiders spun webs between their stalks.

The school on the hill was closed for the holidays, and the bell echoed through the empty building. Mosquitoes and flies glided across the murky surface of its pond.

She went to invigilate an exam and spent the time staring out at the neatly mowed lawn. A flock of birds swooped past, close to the ground. She didn't hear a thing, but saw their black outlines slashing a quick, jagged line through the sky, rising and falling, flapping on the wind, racing to catch insects before the rain. In the distance, a row of manicured trees, and the sky like a low-hanging cloud. The light dimmed, blurring the view, streaking the lawn a dusky yellow. The windows were like paintings.

Before the students arrived, she'd exchanged a few words with a Malay teacher. Purely out of habit, she'd found herself asking: 'Where did you teach before coming here?'

The teacher had answered: 'Malay College University.'

She'd been silent for a while, mulling over each word, as if counting grains of rice. She'd stared into the classroom, at the tables with their place numbers and the rows of empty chairs, and then couldn't help adding: 'When you were there, did you teach any Chinese students?'

The Malay teacher had avoided her eyes. After careful consideration, she'd replied, 'No, the students were all Malay.'

She'd known perfectly well this would be the answer, and yet it shocked her. At the same time, she felt profoundly bored by this routine of asking things to which she knew the answers. Had the question bothered the woman? Perhaps she thought it was hostile, or deliberately provocative? It was impossible to tell; her reply had been perfectly measured. Her eyes gave nothing away. Tone appropriate, expression neutral. Calm as a millpond.

Then the Malay teacher had changed the subject, and started

talking about the student who'd been caught cheating a few days before. He was being expelled, of course. There was a sad resignation to the woman's tone. She had hummed and nodded in response, none of it meaning anything. She thought of this as she continued to stare out of the windows, watching as the rain beat down and the lawn turned hazy.

The air conditioning was very cold and she'd woken up too early. She yawned.

She'd always liked the Malay word *air muka*, used to mean 'facial expression', but literally meaning 'surface of water'. The expression on your face, giving away the emotions beneath. Although in reality, perhaps a rippled surface said more about the wind outside.

Talking. There were appropriate topics, and others it was better not to mention. Some people never seemed to waver over which was which.

Things hidden underwater should not be exposed to air. People laughed, but the loudest never laughed with their eyes. Their eyes were as guarded as nutshells, and their expressions were like caves: you knew at a glance that nothing would slip past them. But knowing was one thing. Knowing could not protect against moments of weakness. For example, forgetting what was appropriate. Forgetting to be vigilant. Because once you forgot, once you'd crossed that line, no matter how you tried to fix things, you'd never make them right again. You'd become gradually more isolated. Up until now, the line had always been very clear.

She started to feel bored of herself, and bored of drawing the line.

May came, and the wind turned with the season. She had to remind herself to close the windows before she left work. One day she forgot, and arrived to find a shallow puddle of water in one corner of her office. This was how she discovered that her floor wasn't level.

Damp seeped into the plaster of the walls. The air conditioning was set too low for rainy days. She hunched her shoulders and walked into his office. He was reading a letter and looked up sternly from his desk as she entered, just as he usually did.

'Students tell me you've been promoting homosexuality in your classes?' he said. 'And that you made a Muslim student read a homosexual poem out loud?'

She would have defended herself, but then realised he must be referring to e.e. cummings, and even the thought of trying to explain made her feel so exhausted that in the end she said nothing at all.

'This is an extremely serious matter,' he continued. 'I've received complaints. I'm sure I don't need to spell it out for you, because you know what kind of place this is. There are people who prefer not to encounter these things. Naturally, you can teach whatever you like – and, well, I understand that literature shouldn't be confused with politics . . . but now we have this problem, and it's going to be tricky to explain to the higher-ups. To be frank, if it weren't for the complaint, I'd be inclined to ignore it.'

She was silent.

'One of your students uploaded a video of himself online. There he is, on the internet, reading this poem of yours, making a speech about coming out of the closet. You should take a look, count up the death threats in the comments . . .

'Believe me, I wish they weren't taking this so seriously. I don't know what the committee will have to say about it. If they do decide to make a fuss – if they start picking through the egg yolk for bones, so to speak – they're going to want an explanation. You'll have to start thinking about what to say.'

Her preferred option was to say nothing and have the issue quietly fade away. There was a stack of documents on his desk, the top one branded with an intricate seal. The red stamped wax was like an omen, but one too mysterious for her to decipher.

Outside the office, it was so intensely quiet that she felt her eardrums might burst. She went to the canteen, where she met the Malay teacher from the day of the exam. They waved at one another, both smiling weakly. Did this woman know? And if she did, was she the kind of person who liked to make trouble and would go spreading it about?

She was distracted all afternoon, arriving ten minutes late to her class, teaching half-heartedly. Her brain was like a miswired electric circuit. She filled in paperwork incorrectly and had to start again, and then again.

At dinner time, the house filled with the blare of the television. Soap opera, adverts, news, another soap opera. Her parents looked listlessly at the screen, looked listlessly at her. Or perhaps they were perfectly contented, or mostly contented; she couldn't tell. Then her father stopped watching television and insisted on talking, his eyes fixed on her, asserting his authority. She was his best audience. In these lonely, twilight years, she was the only remaining link between him and the outside world; between him and his fondly remembered days as a primary school headmaster. He didn't approve of her mother's approach to life. Her mother said people had to accept the hand they'd been dealt. That was just how things were. She'd been saying so for decades.

She helped her mother clear the plates, listening patiently to her as they washed up. Her mother's solitary life: to her, life was always someone else's story.

Everything about it. Someone. Else's. Story.

When she was finally alone, she just sat there, loath to move. She couldn't face getting into bed or cleaning her teeth, just wanted to carry on sitting. It occurred to her to look up that video online, and she started trying out keywords in her search bar. Eventually it appeared, but all she could see was the title, because the contents had been blocked.

That line: THIS VIDEO IS A GRAVE THREAT TO THE SAFETY OF OTHERS. IT HAS BEEN REMOVED.

A shiver down her spine.

A week passed, then two. The shivers continued. She carried on going to and from her classroom, still without any thought to how she would explain herself to the committee. In any case, no one summoned her to a meeting. The matter was not mentioned. Had it passed? Been forgotten, just like that? Been hushed up? Or perhaps they'd reached their decision, and no explanations were necessary.

Then, at the end of the month, she heard the news: the committee had dropped her case. They had turned their focus to a younger, more troublesome teacher, who had spoken to a class about the restrictions of the Islamic dress code for women, reportedly claiming it had become conflated with holiness, but was actually rooted in ownership of a woman's body. This had antagonised a few Muslim students, who went to discuss it with the teacher in her office and subsequently pronounced her attitude 'disrespectful of the Quran'. They then wrote a letter of complaint to the head of the department, and the accusations snowballed from there. Coincidentally, the teacher's contract was just about to expire, and the department decided not to renew it.

It had been a busy day and she walked through the campus after class, following the slope, making her habitual detour to the biology department's fish pond. June, and the flame trees were ablaze. She hadn't seen the Malay boy from the drama department again.

Passing along a fluorescent-lit corridor, she came to an open door and couldn't help pausing to look inside. The young Malay teacher was in the middle of packing, the floor strewn with boxes. At the sound of footsteps, she looked up. Waved, said hey.

And so she replied, still outside the door: hey. A twinge of guilt, because while she'd been revelling in her escape, she hadn't given much thought to the reason why.

She hurried in, wanting to be friendly, eager to help, packing tape pulling, ripping, sticking. The woman didn't object. Papers, books in English, books in Malay. A good number of books in Chinese, a few characters on their covers that she could still understand, although she stifled her curiosity. She packed the books into boxes. Then she came to the foil-stamped cover of the Quran, the centre of the storm, and froze. The woman took it from her and slid it nonchalantly into a box, continuing to stack reference books on top.

'Take whatever you like,' she said. 'No one can see us. Even if they could, it would be fine. There's no need to worry.'

The blinds were open and the lights were on. The woman took a pack of cigarettes from her handbag and offered her one, but she shook her head. Holding one in her mouth, the woman bent forward, her hair almost covering her face, and lit it. Tobacco smoke filled the room, irritating her nose and making her nauseous; she imagined her lungs filling with muck.

'I'm very sorry. I heard what happened.' Her words came out haltingly.

'What did you hear?'

'Well, I heard a bit,' she said. 'It wasn't very clear.'

The woman looked at her curiously through the rising coils of smoke. Then she went to sit in her chair, kicking over a pile of magazines so that she could pull it closer to the desk.

'It went like this,' she said, bending forward to open a drawer on the bottom left-hand side of her desk: she mimed taking something out and then, hugging a ball of air to her chest, sat back up and arranged it on her knees. 'They said that when I bent forward, that was against the Quran. It was wrong.'

'Oh. Shit,' she replied, not knowing what she was supposed to say. They had packed up seven or eight boxes.

'We should go. This will take more than one day,' said the woman, taking a final, decisive drag on her cigarette. 'Although the sooner it's done, the better.'

Even after the cigarette had been stubbed out and the ashtray emptied, the smell lingered and she felt it seeping into her clothes and hair.

The end of June shook in her ears.

'Where do you live?' she said, nervously. 'I can drop you. It'll be hard to find a taxi at this time of day.'

The woman lived in the north of the city, in a suburb near the national zoo. She knew the way because she'd been to the zoo before, to look at those lifeless animals in their cages. For the whole car journey, she felt her attention drawn to her left. They didn't exactly know each other, but neither were they complete strangers. Their offices were a few rooms apart and they had often passed one another in the corridor, gone to the same meetings, waited for one another to hand over classes. And now the woman was being singled out as an example. It was hard to fathom. She knew she should keep quiet, was aware the woman wasn't in the best mood, but they still had an hour to go. She started chatting about this and that, making fun of some stupid TV show, complaining about public transport being as crap as ever. Then a press conference came on the radio and they both fell silent, listening as someone attacked the administration for being a festering pile of rubbish.

'What will you do next?' she asked, from the driver's seat.

Her passenger shrugged. 'Don't know.'

'What did they say to you?'

'They're smarter about these things now. It was all very civilised. They said my contract was up. That courses are being restructured and the faculty is moving in a new direction, so my services are no longer required. They didn't mention anything about student complaints.'

'So that's how they played it. I guess you can't argue with that.'

'Argue what?'

She didn't reply.

'Argue that I'm the victim here? Because that's not what I want.'

Things were more complicated than that, she added. Much more complicated than that.

The after-work traffic was like a tide, car after car after car stretching along the outer ring road, all six lanes blocked in like a huge open-air car park. Horns blasted impatiently. The cars inched forward, queuing for the better part of an hour just to pass through the toll booth. In the shimmer of the setting sun, they were part of a sea that stretched all the way to the horizon.

'I might apply to go abroad, if I can find a course,' said the woman, without much enthusiasm. 'What about you? Things are fine now, I take it? You can stay.'

She gave a small, hesitant nod, and then shook her head.

'I don't know, I hope so. Really hope so.' Her voice was strained.

'I saw the video. It's nothing to do with you, some people just love to talk shit,' said the woman. 'English literature has nothing to do with it. They have nothing better to do than intimidate people, and try to make examples.'

She listened quietly, at a loss for words. She was sure that the woman was speaking the truth. But what was true had nothing whatsoever to do with what was safe. The two things were miles apart. Truth was further from safety than two islands at opposite ends of the Earth.

They arrived and waved goodbye. Exhausted, with nothing left to say, she drove off quickly and headed home.

The car turned off the ring road and climbed uphill, entering the vast wooded area that spanned the north of the city. The last rays of sunlight lingered over the treetops, and the narrow road snaked through dark tree trunks and their hazy shadows. Shrubs and branches melded into walls of greenery on either side until, abruptly, they gave way to a wall of billboards. A whole row of advertising for real estate.

It was here that the animal sprang out of nowhere – an elk, or at least something a lot like an elk, appearing all of a sudden outside the window on the driver's side.

Those marvellous antlers. It raced past, the forest trailing behind. Perhaps it wasn't an elk; perhaps just an ordinary deer. She couldn't be sure because biology had never been her strong point.

She couldn't see the whole thing, just parts of it, flashes of head and body, bobbing frantically up and down as it ran, as though being chased by a wild beast. Or as though jumping for joy, just released from a cage. For a few seconds, she completely forgot that she was driving, and couldn't tear her eyes away: such a creature, and for it to have come so near! Right outside her window, silky fur so close she could have touched it. Antlers within easy reach. These were shorter and smaller than the antlers she'd seen on television; a little like broken branches, as though battered by the elements, left hardened and grey. Its neck was long, and its eyes seemed to stare straight at her from the sides of its head, even while it was running away at full pelt, towards something she did not know and could not see.

Briefly, they ran together along the silent road, the shadows of the trees sheltering them like a nest. In the ink-blue twilight, it was as if she'd crossed into a dream world, her everyday consciousness peeled back and replaced by a new, peculiar sensitivity that surged like a wave, so powerful that she felt she might fly. Might leave the surface of the Earth, be swept beyond the horizon and no longer belong to any time, or any place.

It was just a split-second thing. Then there was a giant bend and the car spun and she snapped awake, slamming on the brakes. The wheels screeched. The animal overtook the car, continuing its elegant, carefree sprint around the bend. One second and it had abandoned her, becoming a shrinking grey dot at the end of the road.

The car leapt the kerb, left the road and charged into the wasteland that surrounded the lake. It was over before she could scream.

She came slowly to her senses, and found herself still in her seat. Gingerly, she checked the rear-view mirror and, seeing no cars on the road behind, began a slow reverse. Her back wheels jammed in a muddy ditch. No matter how the engine roared, they would only spin in place.

She turned off the engine. A cloud of mosquitoes flew up, and her ears flooded with an insect whine. The flickering gleam of the water. She could make out a pile of abandoned furniture. There was a sofa right at the edge of the lake – close enough that, if you sat on it, you could surely touch the water with your toe. It was an enticing prospect, beckoning to her like a holiday, but when she walked closer, she realised it was impossible to reach. It was surrounded by old wood and assorted junk. She examined this collection of messy, damp objects, hoping to find planks to put under her wheels.

The mosquitoes attacked her arms and legs. She returned to the car and restarted the engine, but it was no good. She remained trapped as the sky and the lake turned completely black, desperately trying to phone for help. There was no reception; all she heard was the electronic recording from the service provider, over and over again.

She felt wild with frustration. There wasn't a single street light.

She knew that she was some distance from the lake. But she couldn't see anything; her eyes were wide and she couldn't see. The absolute darkness distorted her perspective. She thought of those creation myths and their revered heroes, tearing order from chaos; of their incredible courage. Their astonishment when they saw the first ray of light, and discovered they had eyes. She knew all she had to do was turn on her headlights, but couldn't decide which was safer: to alert others to her existence, or continue to hide in the dark?

She sat quietly for a moment, listening carefully. Listening to the unfamiliar noises out there in the night, the jagged harmony of the trees and insects. Confronting the pitch-black chaos. The wind gusted across the lake. She heard it blowing across her car, through the shrubs and the undergrowth, and she had the weary thought: that's how it is, that's how it is. Now rest for a while. ∎

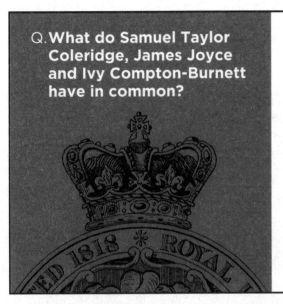

© GUS PALMER
Harlow, 2018

NEW TOWN BLUES

Jason Cowley

Photography by Gus Palmer

1

The three men had been drinking for several hours by the time they arrived at The Stow shopping centre in Harlow. It was approaching midnight on a warm bank holiday weekend towards the end of August. Arkadiusz Jozwik and his two companions – the men were Polish and lived and worked locally in the troubled Essex town – were hungry and tired. Jozwik bought a pizza from a takeaway and sat on a wall to eat it. It was then that he and his companions noticed a group of teenagers nearby, some of them on bikes. The boys, and they were boys, aged fifteen and sixteen, approached and there was a confrontation. The men became loud and antagonistic, and, as each group goaded the other, one of the boys slipped out of the pack and sneaked up behind Jozwik, landing to the back of his head what would later be described in court as his 'Superman punch'.

Jozwik fell – perhaps partly because he was drunk, perhaps partly because he was off balance – and hit his head hard on the pavement, after which the boys panicked and fled. Jozwik was unconscious and blood leaked from his ears as he was taken by ambulance to the town's Princess Alexandra Hospital, from where he was transferred to Addenbrooke's in Cambridge.

The next day Essex police described the attack as 'brutal' and called it a 'potential hate crime' – the suggestion being that Jozwik was assaulted because he was heard speaking Polish. Which alerted the media that what had happened on the night of Saturday 27 August 2016 at The Stow shopping centre was more sinister than a routine late-night altercation that had gone seriously wrong. It was a hate crime, a political crime.

This was the febrile summer of the European referendum when the air was rancid with accusation and counter-accusation and England had never seemed more divided between those who wanted the United Kingdom to continue as a member of the European Union and those who wanted out; between 'Remainers' and 'Leavers'. Like hundreds of thousands of other Poles who had moved to Britain in the years after former Communist states from Eastern Europe joined the EU, Jozwik, who was single, believed life in England offered opportunities that his home country could not. In 2012 he followed his mother, a widow, to Essex because he did not want to be alone in Poland. He lived with her in Harlow, where he found work in a sausage factory.

The day after the attack in The Stow six youths were arrested on suspicion of attempted murder. Then, on 29 August, Arkadiusz Jozwik – Arek to friends and family – died in hospital, having never regained consciousness. He was forty years old and had suffered a brain injury and a fractured skull.

No one has established the exact motivation for the attack – a witness reported that Jozwik racially abused one of the boys, who was black or mixed race – but whatever the motive, the impact of the punch that felled Jozwik was felt around the world: the *New York Times* incorrectly reported, for instance, that he was 'repeatedly pummeled and kicked by a group of boys and girls'. And soon it was being called the 'Brexit Murder'.

Every district in Essex voted Leave in the referendum of 23 June 2016 (the pro-Brexit vote in Harlow, which has high unemployment and areas of deprivation, was 68 per cent compared with the national average of 52 per cent). After Jozwik's death, the Polish president

Andrzej Duda wrote to religious leaders in Britain requesting their assistance in preventing further attacks on Polish nationals and the Polish ambassador to Britain was taken on a tour of Harlow. Around the same time, Polish police officers were sent from Warsaw to patrol the area around The Stow, and the Polish community organised a solidarity march in the town.

'We Europeans can never accept Polish workers being beaten up, harassed or even murdered in the streets of Essex,' the President of the European Commission, Jean-Claude Juncker, said in an annual state of the union address on 14 September.

The subtext of Juncker's intervention was this: the death of Arkadiusz Jozwik was a manifestation of the xenophobic forces unleashed by the Brexit referendum, and Harlow and its people were implicated.

2

Sometimes I dream about Harlow. I was born in what was then called the new town, at home, in a rented maisonette above a parade of shops, with just a midwife to keep watch on my mother as my father waited anxiously with my four-year-old sister in another room. I was educated at various state schools in the town and lived there for the first eighteen years of my life.

In these dreams of Harlow I am who I am now – middle-aged, a husband and father – but I'm invariably back in the house in the quiet cul-de-sac where we lived as a family of five from 1972 to 1983 and where I spent most of my childhood and adolescence before my parents, unsettled by what they considered to be the inexorable decline of the town, moved to Hertfordshire. My father, lucid and calm as he ever was, is alive in these dreams, and I have a sense of having the conversations that his sudden death from a heart attack at the age of fifty-six never allowed us to have.

There was a time, when I first began working in London in my mid-twenties, that I never wanted to be reminded of where I grew up. I could scarcely admit that I was an Essex man, Harlow-born. There was a blockage. A desire to forget or escape. It was as if I was embarrassed about something I couldn't quite articulate, something bound up with the gradations of the English class system and people's perceptions of Harlow as a failed town, as 'Chav Town'.

3

L ocated at the junction of First Avenue and Howard Way, The Stow opened in the early 1950s as the first of the town's neighbourhood shopping centres. But, as with so many of Harlow's public and civic spaces, it has been neglected. I know The Stow well. Our family dentist had his surgery there and, when I was in primary school, after each visit to see him, my mother would treat me to a hot sausage roll or sugar-encrusted jam doughnut from Dorringtons, a family bakery which today still occupies the same space in the two-tier shopping centre, close to where Arkadiusz Jozwik was punched, fell and hit his head.

When I returned to The Stow last April, drawn back by my interest in the 'Brexit Murder', I was shocked at how run-down it was. In the pedestrian-only precinct, pound and charity shops – the RSPCA and Salvation Army occupied what were once prime sites – and scrappy fast-food joints proliferated. There was a tattoo and body-piercing shop. A Thai massage parlour was adjacent to an undertaker, a nice juxtaposition of sex and death that would have amused Freud. The Essex Skipper – the original pubs in the town were named after butterflies or moths just as some of the roads were later renamed after left-wing political heroes, Mandela Avenue, Allende Avenue and so on – was shabby and unwelcoming.

It was an unseasonably warm afternoon yet the area seemed desolate. When I returned to my car three young men were sitting on a wall next to it. One of them introduced himself by saying, 'Good car!' He spoke heavily accented English. He and his friends turned out to be Romanians and when I asked what life was like for Eastern

Europeans in the town they weren't interested in telling me. So I asked if they worked. They said they did not. How long had they been here? Not long. They had believed they were coming to a new town. But, they said, Harlow wasn't new: it looked old.

4

My parents arrived in Harlow in 1959 when there were fewer than 6,000 people there (today the population is 86,000 and rising). They were from east London and had been child wartime evacuees, an experience of separation and dislocation my mother found especially upsetting. Their education was interrupted by the war and they both left school at fifteen, my father (who passed up a scholarship to study engineering) to work as an apprentice shirt-cutter and my mother as an assistant in a City of London law firm. They met at a dance at Manor Hall, Chigwell, Essex, and were married in 1958. A few months later they moved to Harlow – my mother's eldest sister had already settled there – searching for new opportunities in the nascent new town.

The 1946 New Towns Act created eight towns, the purpose of which was to provide decent housing for 340,000 'surplus' or 'bombed-out' Londoners – after more than a million houses were destroyed or damaged in the capital during the Second World War. Most of them were already small country towns – Hemel, Stevenage, Hatfield, Welwyn – that would be extended or built around. But Harlow in rural west Essex would be completely new – 60 per cent of the land was compulsorily purchased from one owner, Commander Godfrey Arkwright, the head of an old Essex hunting and landowning family – and the first arrivals there considered themselves pioneers, marking out new territory.

The original village of Harlow (renamed Old Harlow) is mentioned in the Domesday Book. This and other long-established settlements – Potter Street, Parndon, Netteswell, Tye Green, Latton, Churchgate Street – were subsumed by the chief architect-planner

Frederick Gibberd into his urban masterplan: built on and around, developed, expanded but not erased or demolished. It was essential for Gibberd that Harlow combined town and country, the urban and rural: he wanted open countryside inside and surrounding the town. He wanted to create 'a fine contrast between the work of man and the work of God'. The valley of the River Stort formed the northern boundary and, as Gibberd wrote, 'small hamlets and fine woods [were] interspersed throughout the area'.

My parents were delighted by how rural Harlow was when they arrived: the town was being built around them, self-contained neighbourhood by neighbourhood. For the first time in his life my father suffered from hay fever, which blighted his summers but mysteriously disappeared whenever he returned for any length of time to the city or travelled overseas.

For my parents moving to Harlow was a form of escape: away from the bomb sites and ruined Victorian buildings and streets of east London and, they believed, towards a more optimistic future. From the old to the new. Lord Reith, the first Director General of the BBC, was chairman of the New Towns Committee. For Reith, these towns were 'essays in civilisation', and he wanted the people in them to have 'a happy and gracious way of life'.

The emphasis in Harlow in the early years was always on the new – on new hope, new beginnings and on the vitality of youth. Don't look back. Never look back. Yet, in the 1960s, there were reports of a phenomenon that became known as 'new town blues' – the experience of dislocation and isolation felt by those who were struggling to adapt or who simply mourned the loss of the communities from which they'd been deracinated.

But I knew nowhere else. By the time I was born, Harlow was known as 'pram town' because of all the young couples starting families there, and the birth rate was three times higher than the national average. Henry Moore, whose house and studio were in the nearby Hertfordshire hamlet of Perry Green, was invited to create a public sculpture that symbolised the radiant promise of the new town.

Today, Moore's *Harlow Family Group* is situated in the expansive entrance area to the town's civic centre. A man and woman sit side by side, proud and upright. The man's right arm is wrapped protectively around the woman and she is holding a young child. At its unveiling outside St Mary-at-Latton Church, Mark Hall, in 1956, Sir Kenneth Clark, then chairman of the Arts Council of Great Britain, called Moore's sculpture, which is 2.5 metres high and weighs 1.5 tonnes, a symbol of a 'new humanitarian civilisation' that had emerged out of the devastation of the Second World War.

Harlow Family Group was one of many notable pieces by Barbara Hepworth, Leon Underwood, Ralph Brown, Elisabeth Frink, Gerda Rubinstein, Auguste Rodin, Karel Vogel and others bought and commissioned by the Harlow Arts Trust, which was set up in 1953 and supported by philanthropists and the town corporation. It was paternalistic, this desire to create public art for ordinary working people, but the motivation was pure. 'So often sculpture is a sort of cultural concession that has little relevance to the real life of a town but, in [this] case, it has become an integral part of Harlow,' Frederick Gibberd said in 1964. He wanted Harlow to be 'home to the finest works of art, as in Florence and other splendid cities'.

5

This was an era – hard to believe now – when London was depopulating. Before he was married my father, the only child of a bus driver, lived in a terraced house in Forest Gate, which, as the name suggests, is where the East End thins out and nudges up against Epping Forest. The family home had a small garden and outside lavatory. My father was a talented boy and a gifted cricketer, and he and his mother were frustrated by the life that was being mapped out for him (his father, Frank, who boxed recreationally in the East End pubs, was a quiet, kindly, unambitious man). He did not want to follow his father onto the buses or work in the docks as some of his ancestors had. Nor did he want to emigrate to Australia, like one of his uncles. My father was culturally aspirational. Encouraged by his fiercely protective, austere, red-haired mother (she used to wear a brooch displaying a photograph of her son, whom she called 'everyone's favourite'), he dressed smartly, read poetry, listened to jazz music and bought the *Observer* every Sunday for the books and arts reviews. He liked the theatre and was enchanted by Hollywood. He adored the Marx Brothers and W.C. Fields. The East End of his late adolescence was not today's vibrant, polyglot, multi-ethnic realm of hipster bars, tech start-ups, barista masterclasses, Balti curry houses, craft-beer festivals, Tinder and Grindr hook-ups, and astronomical property prices: it was parochial, impoverished and diminished. He wanted out.

Yet something happened to my father in middle age, a period when his good career in what he always called the 'rag trade' seemed to drift and stall, and he became increasingly nostalgic and introspective. He began to brood on the old world he'd left behind as a young man – the sense of community he'd known, the neighbourliness. Perhaps very belatedly he, too, was suffering from new town blues. He listened repeatedly to music from the 1940s, especially the popular songs of Al Bowlly, the southern African crooner killed by a German parachute bomb that exploded outside his London flat in 1941. 'Oh, no, he's going on about the war years again,' we used to tease. He showed me some of the poems he wrote, always set in the East End during the early 1940s or just at the end of the war. One was called 'Don't Cheer Us Girls We're British', an ironic slogan he'd seen written on a jeep carrying troops along a road close to where he lived.

My father was a war child. The first day of the Blitz, 7 September 1940 – 'Black Saturday' – a day of clear blue skies, coincided with his sixth birthday. He was so traumatised by the experience of the assault on the docklands and nearby neighbourhoods – he recalled burning buildings and an apocalyptic red glow in the sky – that he lost his voice. His father, the bus driver, refused to leave the house during subsequent intense bombing raids. My father and his mother would hurry to an air-raid shelter whenever they heard the sirens warning of an imminent Luftwaffe attack; but Frank would try his luck above ground, even as nearby houses and buildings were being destroyed.

Towards the end of his life, my father spoke often about how the depredations but also the intensity of a child's experience of the home front, and indeed of the urgency of wartime more generally, united the people around him: there was a commonality of purpose, a conviction that if they could endure, if they could get through the worst, the future would be better. Which is why Harlow seemed so attractive to him.

War and the wartime command economy (Labour leader Clement Attlee officially became Churchill's deputy prime minister in the coalition government in February 1942, though he was the effective deputy as Lord Privy Seal from May 1940) created the conditions for socialism and a new settlement in Britain. Without the war, the Labour Party would not have swept to power in 1945. 'The revolution in England has already begun,' H.G. Wells said on 22 May 1940 when Attlee introduced the Emergency Powers Defence Bill in the House of Commons and sandbags went up across Westminster. For George Orwell, who admired the patriotism of the working class, the 'English revolution' gathered momentum with the epic retreat from Dunkirk. 'Like all else in England, it happens in a sleepy, unwilling way, but it is happening,' Orwell wrote. 'The war has speeded it up, but it has also increased, and desperately, the necessity for speed.'

6

To grow up in Harlow was to be on the front line of the English revolution. More than this, you were a cog in a grand social and political experiment. I understand this now but back then I was just living. My friends and I were children of the welfare state. The social transformations and central planning of the immediate post-war period, as the new Labour government set about building what Attlee called a 'New Jerusalem', had created thrilling possibilities for us. The National Health Service was established; the National

Insurance Act abolished the hated means test for welfare provision; essential industries such as the railways and mining were nationalised; the Town and Country Planning Act was passed, opening the way for mass housebuilding and the redevelopment of huge tracts of land; Britain's independent nuclear deterrent was commissioned; the gap between rich and poor narrowed.

This was a very British revolution, and a pragmatic experiment with socialism: the state was powerful but not all-powerful. It was not a vindictive exercise in destruction but one of creation: about a new social contract between the state and the individual to enhance the common good. The monarchy, the landowning families and the ancient public schools (Attlee was a proud Haileyburian) were untouched. Individual freedom and the great British institutions were cherished. The cost of war had impoverished the nation, left it with a ruinous trade deficit and ended Britain's imperial hegemony. But these were new times. Progressive change was not only possible, it was believed to be necessary. As Attlee recognised, the British people 'wanted a new start'. They had suffered and they had endured. Now, he said, they were 'looking towards the future'.

Our lives as children were socially engineered and it seemed everything we needed was provided by the state: housing, education, health care, libraries, recreational and sports facilities. There were so-called playschemes (quasi-summer camps) where we gathered to play or take part in organised games during the holidays. The town had a network of cycle tracks, among the most extensive in the country, which connected all neighbourhoods to the high-density town centre, the High, which was built on the highest settlement, and to the two main industrial areas, Temple Fields and the Pinnacles. In 1961, a multi-purpose sports centre, the first of its kind in Britain, was opened. It was funded by local people through voluntary contributions via their rates (my aunt was proud to be one of the enthusiastic contributors).

One friend has since described the experience of growing up in the town in the sixties and seventies as 'East Germany without the

Stasi'. Those of us born and raised there were referred to as 'citizens of the future'. Rural spaces (the so-called green wedges of the master plan, one of which became the magnificent town park, with its skating rink, bandstand, nine-hole pitch and putt golf course and animal centre) and planned recreation areas for children were meant to encourage us to lead healthy, active lives and to play in safety. In the words of the 1958 public information film about Harlow, 'If these boys and girls don't grow up to face successfully the problems of their day, it will not be the fault of the architects and planners who helped to give them a start.'

7

W hat I didn't realise then – of course, I saw but I did not see – was that Harlow was, in effect, a monoculture. The original aspiration was to create a 'classless' society but, growing up there, it felt mostly as if you were living in a one-class town – that was, working class. There was a small middle-class intelligentsia, who participated in Labour Party politics, in the local drama, literary and film societies and who gathered around the Playhouse, which had opened in 1971 for live theatre, films and exhibitions. My father, whose interests were cultural rather than political, was part of this scene.

But, on the whole, nearly everyone I met was white working class. Out of the 250 or so children in my year at secondary school – a huge non-selective, mixed-ability comprehensive, opened in 1959 and enlarged in 1972, one of eight in the town – I remember one boy whose family was Hong Kong Chinese (he ended up running an oriental restaurant in Germany) and two girls whose parents were Indian. Everyone else was white. My classmates' parents had, for the most part, come from the East End or the poorer parts of north London, such as Edmonton or Walthamstow, and many worked in the town's factories and manufacturing plants – the International Telephone and Telegraph Corporation (which by the end of the 1970s employed 8,000 people), the Cossor Group, Revertex Chemicals,

Johnson Matthey Metals, Schreiber, Pitney Bowes, United Glass. These companies had their own social clubs and sports teams, even boys' football teams, which I played against in the recreational league for Newtown Spartak, a name more redolent of the Soviet Union.

Before the introduction of Margaret Thatcher's Right to Buy scheme, which enabled tenants to buy their council house at a large discount, most of the houses in the town were owned by the town corporation. (Even today, a third of the housing stock is council-owned.) Yet from 1972 we owned our house, and lived on one of the few private developments, or executive estates as they were known. This set us apart somewhat. This and the fact that my father did not work locally but commuted to London, driving there in his Alfa Romeo rather than take the train. Because he worked in the rag trade – designing, range-building, merchandising – he wore fashionable, often flamboyant clothes, and he travelled incessantly – to India, Hong Kong, the United States, South Korea, France, Switzerland, Italy, Germany.

My father had studied at night school and was unusually articulate – 'posh' my friends called him. But he wasn't posh: he simply did not speak with the local accent, which today we call 'Estuary English', the dialect associated with people living in and around London, especially close to the River Thames and its estuary. My mother called it 'sub-cockney', distinguishing it from the accent of her father, a hard-working and thrifty carpenter who was born, as she liked to remind us, 'within the sound of the Bow Bells' (the bells of St Mary-le-Bow church, Cheapside), a badge of honour worn by true cockneys.

Daily life at my secondary school was a process of negotiation and adaptation: I could not speak there as freely and candidly as I did at home. At home, if I spoke as I did at school, my mother would chasten me for my glottal stops and h-dropping. At school, if I spoke as I did at home, I would have been mocked as 'posh', a grave insult. If some of my classmates visited our book-cluttered house, I used to hide my father's magazines – the *New Statesman*, the *Listener*, *i-D*, *City Limits* – and newspapers because he did not read the *Sun* or the *Mirror*, like their fathers. I was frustrated that he did not conform to

Harlow norms, even though the conformity I wished upon him would have been a betrayal of all that he wanted, who he was, his great expectations. Sometimes when he was out I'd open his wardrobe and be overwhelmed by the warm, seductive smell of his clothes. I was especially fascinated by his two-colour shoes and exotic shirts and bright ties. Why did he dress so unlike my classmates' fathers, some of whom wore donkey jackets and DM boots to work?

There was little sense, in the five years I spent at comprehensive school (I left at the age of sixteen to do A levels at Harlow College), that we were being prepared for university. I once mentioned, on a whim, that I'd like to study law without knowing what that would have entailed. I was told by a teacher that law was for 'private-school boys', as if that was the end of the matter. *It was useful to get that learnt.* Most weeks it was a case of getting through and getting by. Woodwork, metalwork, motor vehicle studies and home economics were among the subjects taught. I was hopeless at all of them.

8

My father liked to remind us that we owed our opportunities as citizens of the future to the idealism of the war generation. But progress isn't inevitable. There's no guarantee that things will keep getting better, that the arc of history bends towards enlightenment. History isn't linear but, I think, contingent and discontinuous, even cyclical. Ron Bill, an associate of my mother who worked for the Harlow Development Corporation, once told me that he and his colleagues had reached for Utopia. 'The town attracted progressives, community-minded people,' he said. 'Frederick Gibberd was an example of such a person. That first wave of people who came to the town in the fifties and sixties – many of them socialists and communists – they wanted to build something. The trouble is, there wasn't a second wave equal to the first.'

Utopia means nowhere or no place. Harlow is often called a nowhere zone or left-behind town, which you pass through on the way to somewhere else. *News from Nowhere* was the title of William Morris's futuristic novel about a socialist Utopia. There was only bad news from Harlow following Arkadiusz Jozwik's death in the summer of 2016. The suggestion in much of the initial reporting of the so-called Brexit Murder was that in reaching for Utopia the town's pioneers and planners had ended up creating the opposite of what was intended: a dystopia.

9

On 31 July 2017, I went to Chelmsford Crown Court to hear Judge Patricia Lynch deliver her verdict on the Jozwik case. Before proceedings began I sat in a tatty reception area outside the courtroom directly opposite to where the teenage defendant's family waited. Almost a year had passed since Arkadiusz Jozwik had died, and the defendant, who could not be named for legal reasons, was now sixteen. His family – including his mother and grandmother – were suspicious of my interest and did not want to be interviewed when I approached them. The youth just looked at me blankly. I gave the family my contact details and asked if they would call me, but they never did. I followed up with several phone calls to their solicitor in Old Harlow. But the family had chosen silence.

That afternoon I spoke to the defendant's uncle as he smoked a cigarette in the sunshine outside the court building. He was in his twenties, had a sleeve of tattoos on one arm and expressed bewilderment about what had happened at The Stow. Inside, the youth wore a white shirt several sizes too big, a loosely knotted thick dark tie and plain black trousers. He was short, had a wavy fringe and a wispy moustache. He seemed lost and, at times, even bored as he sat in the box, watched anxiously by his mother. She had a heavy cold, though it was high summer, and I noticed her nails were bitten down to stubs.

The mother looked sadly unsurprised as her son was convicted by a jury of the manslaughter of Arkadiusz Jozwik. Jenny Hopkins,

Chief Crown Prosecutor, said she was satisfied that there had been
no intent by the youth to kill Jozwik. It was not a racist attack or hate
crime, as had been widely reported. 'We decided therefore that the
correct charge was one of manslaughter,' she said. 'Manslaughter is
the unlawful killing of another person with an intention to do some
harm or the foresight that some physical harm may result. The court
was told the youth put 'the full force of his body into the punch' and
he must have been aware when 'he punched Mr Jozwik in this way
that some harm was likely to be caused'.

The Chief Prosecutor continued, 'This was a senseless assault
and with that one punch, which was over in seconds, the youth was
responsible for Mr Jozwik losing his life and causing unimaginable
anguish to Mr Jozwik's family and friends.'

The judge announced that sentencing would take place on Friday
8 September. By this time, the media were losing interest in the case.
This was no 'Brexit Murder'.

10

One rainy morning just before Christmas, I went to see the head
of Harlow Council, an animated Labour councillor called
Jon Clempner. He was angry at how, in his view, Essex police had
mishandled the case, allowing the fires of rumour and allegation to
rage out of control. (Clempner resigned as leader in January 2018.)
'The police knew within twenty-four hours that it was not a racist
attack or a murder. But they did not close down the speculation until
it was too late,' he told me as we drank tea. His office was in the civic
centre overlooking the Water Gardens, which were originally designed
by Frederick Gibberd as a series of parallel terraces and have since
been reconfigured and truncated. From the wide, high window, I
looked out across the Water Gardens, over a car park, cycle track, some
woodland and nearby fields. Beyond these fields I could see in the far
distance the housing estate where my grandfather came to live after he
retired, so that he could be closer to his son, who would die before him.

Something was missing, however: the high-rise modernist town hall, once considered to be Harlow's most important building in its most important space, the civic square. Designed by Gibberd and opened by Clement Attlee in 1960, it was demolished in the mid-2000s as part of the first phase of the redevelopment of the semi-derelict town centre. A huge Asda supermarket now dominated the space where the town hall once stood in imposing isolation, like a monumental watchtower.

One afternoon, many years ago, while on a school trip to the High when I still lived in the town, some friends and I detached ourselves from the group and slipped illicitly into the town hall. Local rumour had it that there was a nuclear bunker in the basement and we wanted to find it. But, instead, we took the lift up to the observation tower where we found ourselves quite alone. We looked out across the surrounding landscape. There, laid out before us, were the cool, clean geometric patterns of the town in which we lived, with its centrally planned network of roads and avenues, its schools and factories and council estates and green wedges. We remained in the observation tower until it was almost dark, watching in wonder as the lights in the distant houses below were switched on, one by one, their amber shimmer illuminating the grid-like structures on which the town was built. And then the houses seemed to melt away and I tried to imagine what it must have been like here before the new town came, the rural tranquillity and the emptiness, the very absence of people.

11

It's taken me a long time to recalibrate the experience of growing up in Harlow. Most of the children I knew, some clever and gifted, never considered for a moment that university was a possibility for them and they contentedly left full-time education as soon as they could. Who knows what became of them.

Like most of my peers, I very nearly didn't make it to university.

I rebelled at Harlow College, switching subjects and missing or repeatedly turning up late for classes, before eventually dropping out. In my late teens, after signing on the dole, restlessly bored, in love with someone who was in love with someone else and in need of money, I found a job as a clerk at the Electricity Council, at Millbank in London. I couldn't afford the train fare so commuted on a coach from my parents' house, a journey that took two or three hours on some days because of traffic congestion. And then you had to do it again in the evening. But it was during those coach journeys that I began reading seriously for the first time.

After six months working as a clerk in a labyrinthine public-sector bureaucracy, I decided to cram-study A levels. In other words, I gave myself nine months to change my life. A benevolent senior manager at the Electricity Council allowed me 'day release' from the office every Friday to return to Harlow College, where I'd been such a poor student and mocked as a 'dilettante' by my tutor. This time, I would study politics, in which I had an intensifying interest. I also enrolled to study for an A level in English literature at a Thursday-evening night class at a comprehensive school in Old Harlow. There, I came under the influence of a man called David Huband, who was wise, soft-voiced and bearded, and the kind of inspirational teacher I'd never encountered before, the *one* teacher we all need to meet. As one of the local intelligentsia he knew people who knew my father and he took an interest in me. He must have sensed that I was in trouble, existentially alarmed and adrift.

The three hours I spent in his company every Thursday evening, from seven to ten, changed how I thought about the world, and those nine months, from September 1985 to May 1986, working at the council, reading while on the coach and studying at weekends at Harlow library or at home, were transformative. I told virtually no one I was studying because I feared failure and the continuing humiliation of life as a clerk. In late May and June, as the football World Cup played out in Mexico, I took my A levels. At the end of the summer I left for university: in one bound, I believed I was finally free from Harlow and all its associations, never looking back. Forward, forward, forward.

12

On 8 September 2017, a sixteen-year-old Harlow resident was sentenced to three and a half years in a young offender institution for the manslaughter of Arkadiusz Jozwik. Passing sentence, Judge Patricia Lynch said that Jozwik had been a 'perfectly decent, well-loved man in his prime'. He would be mourned by his family. As the judge spoke you could hear people in the courtroom weeping. 'A year has passed since Arek died but every day I miss him as much,' Ewa Jozwik, his mother, said in a statement read out in court. 'There are moments I don't want to live any more.' She was present for the sentencing and wept continuously.

For the defence, Patrick Upward said that the youth, who once again wore a white shirt and black tie as he sat in the defendant box, felt 'remorse' at what had happened – he nodded when he heard this – and made reference to his troubled family background and the serious illness of his father. The court heard that he had two previous convictions, one for threatening behaviour, yet was 'not far removed from being a youngster of good character despite those difficulties'. But, in her final address, Judge Lynch said that the defendant had fled the shopping centre after the attack and done 'nothing for the welfare of the deceased'. When the sentence was announced, the youth – who resembled more than ever a lost boy – waved meekly at his family and stumbled slightly as he left the box. His mother, crying now, shouted, 'I love you.' She and other family members hurried out of the courtroom and could be heard weeping in the corridor.

It was raining as Ewa Jozwik left the court building in Chelmsford. Asked by waiting reporters outside, several from Polish television stations, if she believed the sentence was fair, she shook her head in a forlorn gesture of frustration or defeat. 'All the time I can see in my mind the moment I saw him lying motionless in the hospital bed connected to the life-support machine,' she said of her dead son. 'I wanted him to wake up badly.'

Arkadiusz Jozwik is buried in Harlow and the inscription on his gravestone is YOU WERE A DREAM, NOW YOU ARE A MEMORY.

Reflecting on the case, I felt only sorrow – for Jozwik, of course, and those who loved him, but also for the incarcerated youth, 'not far removed from being a youngster of good character', and his family. I felt sorrow, too, for Harlow, which in the immediate aftermath of Jozwik's death, as the town was flooded with reporters from around the world and Polish police patrolled The Stow shopping centre, had come to symbolise all that was perceived to be rotten in England. The vote for Brexit had revealed a fractious and fractured country. Harlow, a once-utopian settlement, was one of the 'left behind' towns, with a disenchanted and xenophobic population. Though only a short thirty-minute train ride from the stupendous wealth and diversity of one of the world's most globalised cities, it had been locked out from prosperity, as if part of another country altogether.

13

One recent afternoon I went on a bike ride around Harlow: the cycle tracks, though more rutted and uneven than before, remain among the glories of the town. I enjoyed being back on a brisk cold day. I know few people there nowadays and visit only very occasionally to see my mother's eldest sister who is ninety. She has lived in the same modest terraced house for more than five decades, a short walk from the first school I attended as an infant. Yet, in recent years, rather than go straight home after visiting my aunt, I've found myself driving around estates I once knew so well, along roads still familiar, past fields where I used to play. Once I pulled up outside the church where I was an altar boy – until playing Sunday-morning football liberated me from the unloved ritual.

I'm not sure what I'm looking for. I once even retraced my

morning walk to secondary school, which involved making my way along a narrow alleyway that ran between the gardens of two houses at the end of which teenage smokers would wait intimidatingly. For amusement or out of boredom they kicked holes in the wooden garden fences and, though they were only one hundred metres or so from the school gates, there were never any teachers around to caution them.

The school closed long ago and is now a business centre, yet, in my imagination, especially since our young son started full-time education four years ago, I can't stop wandering its corridors. On that return visit, as I stood in a car park that had once been our playground, it was as if I could hear the thrilling sound of children's voices all around and, in my chest, I felt the burning sensation of long-dormant frustrations and regrets.

14

Harlow celebrated its seventieth anniversary in 2017 and there are palpable signs of renewal: 10,000 new homes will be built as part of the Gilston Park development as the town expands north of the main train station; Public Health England is building a new science and research campus there which will create thousands of new jobs; an Enterprise Zone is attracting inward investment; the town centre, so boisterous and vibrant, especially on market days, when I was a boy, is set to be redeveloped and will, at last, become fully residential. Harlow is fortuitously situated between London and Cambridge on the M11 corridor. It need not be left behind.

In common with most of the other post-war new towns, Harlow declined, especially after the remit of the Development Corporation ended, because of a lack of capital investment and of the failure to renew its housing estates and its infrastructure. Many of the large factories and manufacturing plants also closed or relocated, creating unemployment. As early as 1953, the *New Statesman* warned that, without greater investment, the new towns would bear 'for the rest of their life the marks of early malnutrition'. It was a prescient observation.

From the beginning, there were flaws in Frederick Gibberd's master plan, most significantly making the town centre non-residential as well as segregating the residential and industrial areas. Town centres thrive when people live and work in them. Some of the council estates, such as Bishopsfield, which was close to where we lived and was known locally as 'the Kasbah' because of its oppressively narrow alleyways, were ideological experiments in modernist design. Less consideration was given to what it was like to live on these brutalist estates, some of which had to be pulled down in later decades because they were built using inadequate materials and failed to meet the government's 'decent homes' standard. Plus, Gibberd did not plan for the preponderance of motor cars, and today many of the small front gardens in the estates have been concreted over to provide space for them.

As an energetic, sports-obsessed boy, so much of what I relished back then – the swimming pool, the sports centre, the playschemes, the pitch and putt in the park, the town hall – was allowed to decay and was then demolished. But perhaps the truth is that the second generation who were born in Harlow and had no experience of wartime or life elsewhere did not believe in the town as their parents had. For them, it just happened to be where they lived, nothing more or less. The children of the idealistic middle class did not, on the whole, stay there: as soon as they could they moved on and out. They moved to London, an inversion of their parents' original journey. There was no second wave of progressives committed to the new town dream. If I once thought I disliked the town or was embarrassed by it, I no longer feel that way. I'm grateful the wartime generation reached for Utopia. My father and mother did the right thing by leaving London when they did. It's worth remembering that Utopia also means good place. Somewhere along the way Harlow ceased to be special. It ceased to be new. But it is not nowhere or no place. It is where I was born and grew up. It is my home town. ∎

© RIBA COLLECTIONS/HERBERT LIONEL WAINWRIGHT
Market Square, Harlow new town, 1957

Market Square, 2018

Town Square and Broad Walk, *c.*1960

Town Square and Broad Walk, 2018

The Stow, *c.*1955

© GUS PALMER
The Stow, 2018

The Stow, 1967

The Stow, 2018

The Lawn, one of the first residential high-rises in England, 1957

The Lawn, now a Grade II-listed building, 2018

Stone Cross, 1950

© GUS PALMER
Stone Cross, 2018

Bishopsfield, *c.* 1968

© GUS PALMER
Bishopsfield, 2018

Will Harris

Holy Man

Everywhere was coming down with Christmas, the streets
and window displays ethereal after rain, but what was it . . .
October? Maybe it was that I'd been thinking about why I hated
Tibetan prayer flags and whether that was similar to how
I felt about Christmas: things become meaningless severed
from the body of ritual, of belief. Then I thought about
those who see kindness in my face, or see it as unusually
calm, which must have to do with that image of the Buddha
smiling. I turned off Regent Street and onto Piccadilly,
then down a side road by Costa to Jermyn Street, where
a man caught my eye as I was about to cross the road
and asked to shake my hand. You have a kind face, he said.

Really. He was wearing a diamond-checked golfer's
jumper and said he was a holy man. As soon as he let go,
he started scribbling in a notepad, then tore out a sheet which
he scrunched into a little ball and pressed to his forehead
and the back of his neck before blowing on it—once, sharply—
and giving it to me. I see kindness in you, but also bad habits.
Am I right? Not drinking or drugs or sex, not like that, but bad
habits. 2019 will be a good year for you. Don't cut your hair
on a Tuesday or Thursday. Have courage. He took out his
wallet and showed me a photograph of a temple, in front
of which stood a family. His, I think. A crowd of businessmen
flowed around us. Name a colour of the rainbow, he said.

Any colour, except red or orange. He was looking to my right,
at what I thought could be a rainbow—despite the sun,
a light wind blew the rain about like scattered sand—but when
I followed his gaze it seemed to be fixed on either a fish
restaurant or a suit display, or maybe backwards in time
to the memory of a rainbow. Why did he stop me? I'd been
dawdling, staring at people on business lunches. Restaurants
like high-end clinics, etherised on white wine. I must
have been the only one to catch his eye, to hold it. What
colour could I see? I tried to picture the full spectrum
arrayed in stained glass, shining sadly, and then refracted
through a single shade that appeared to me in the form

of a freshly mown lawn, a stack of banknotes, a cartoon frog,
a row of pines, an unripe mango, a septic wound. I saw
the glen *beside the tall elm-tree where the sweetbriar smells
so sweet*, then the lane in Devon where my dad grew up,
and the river in Riau where my mum played. It was blue
and yellow mixed, like Howard Hodgkin's version of
a Bombay sunset, or pistachio ice cream; a jade statue of
the Buddha. I remembered being asked—forced—to give
my favourite colour by a teacher (why did it matter?),
which was the colour of my favourite Power Ranger,
of the Knight beheaded by Gawain, of the girdle given
to him by Lady Bertilak, and chose the same again.

The paper in your hand, if it is your colour, will bring you luck,
and if not . . . He trailed off. First hold it to your forehead,
then the back of your neck. Then blow. I unscrunched the ball.
Now put it here, he said, opening his wallet, and money
please. I had no cash. Nothing? He looked me in the eyes and
said (again) that he was a *holy man*. I felt honour-bound
to give him something. Up and down the street, men rode
to their important offices. I told him it was my favourite
colour, or had been, and as I did I saw us from a distance,
as we might seem years from now—scraps of coloured fabric
draped across a hall which, taken out of context, signified
nothing—and I flinched, waiting for the blade to fall.

RENDERINGS

Edward Burtynsky

Introduction by Anthony Doerr

For over three decades, the Canadian photographer and filmmaker Edward Burtynsky has been traveling the planet making astonishing images of landscapes. He takes them with large-format cameras from godlike, elevated positions in remote places like Iceland or the Baja Peninsula or the Niger Delta.

But these are not nostalgic visions of untrammeled nature, destined for office calendars or iPhone backgrounds. No leafy asters bloom against backdrops of sawtoothed peaks; no toucans emerge from dark canopies to wag their bills.

In Burtynsky's landscapes, we see the Earth we live on right now: a place humans have hacked up, carved up, blown up, spilled on and recycled. Bright orange tailings from a nickel mine wind through gray Ontario mud. A canyon of bare dirt twists between walls made by hundreds of thousands of discarded automobile tires. An oil spill spreads a gorgeous blue splotch across the sea.

Burtynsky shows us suburbia pressed against wetlands, supertanker graveyards in Bangladesh and parking lots so big they challenge comprehension. His best photographs are expressionistic, almost calligraphic, as though he's displaying the hidden signatures our collective appetites have etched across the Earth. They are startling, frozen pictures, sometimes remote, sometimes intimate, sometimes both at the same time.

I find them repellent. I also find them beautiful.

*

Not so long ago, a reader waited in a queue to meet me after a public event. The gentleman shook my hand and told me that he enjoyed the *beginning* of a novel I'd written. I braced myself, then did my best to maintain eye contact while he explained that he detested the ending of this particular book (near which one of the protagonists dies).

'What,' he wanted to know, 'was the *purpose*? What was the *point*?'

I'm afraid I mumbled something like, 'I just tried to tell the story as carefully as I could.' But later that night, tossing in my hotel bed, I had so many purposes! So many points! I wished I had told him that I wanted to show how hard war was on the young, how technology can be a force for oppression and for liberation, how all lives, even the smallest, are worth investigating.

I wished I had told him that I had wanted to make something both repellent and beautiful.

*

Often when I stare into the alien circuitry of a Burtynsky picture, it takes me a while to figure out what has actually been photographed. Is that a rock quarry, are those tiny figures people, are those oil pump jacks?

For a moment it becomes a sort of game. And then, after I manage to puzzle out several of his images – a forest of Shanghai skyscrapers, say; then a quilt of Spanish olive groves; then the ruins of a Mexican shrimp farm – I am inevitably confronted by simultaneous awe and despair at the scale of what our industries are doing to the Earth. The pressure that 7.6 billion humans are putting on the planet becomes visual, becomes emotional.

'I want to use my images,' Burtynsky said in his 2005 TED Prize acceptance speech, 'to persuade millions of people to join in the global conversation on sustainability'.

This is not the most fashionable sort of statement for an artist to make. We tend to shy away from any creative work that tries to nudge us in a political direction, particularly if it's in a direction we're not already traveling. If art tries to be moral, goes the argument, then it's not artful. It's didactic.

Here's Garrison Keillor, from his introduction to *Best American Short Stories 1998*: 'A story that carries its lesson under its arm is immediately distrusted.'

Here's Mary Gordon writing in the *Atlantic* in 2005: 'I believe that if your primary motivation in life is to be moral, you don't become an artist. You do good works.'

And yet, doesn't the elevation of certain images or certain stories over other images or other stories involve moral judgment? Each time we arrange things within a frame (whether the frame of a camera lens or the boards of a book) don't we, simply by the acts of inclusion and exclusion, make a near-infinity of moral calculations?

Do Burtynsky's photographs make you think about scarcity and abundance? Do they make you reconsider the life cycles of the stuff around you – your home, your computer, your shoes, your toaster, your olives, your popcorn shrimp? That's up to you.

What's the *purpose*? What's the *point*?

I should have told that gentleman the same thing Burtynsky's photos say to me every time I see them.

Look at this, the pictures say. See this. This is happening. This is where you live. ∎

I

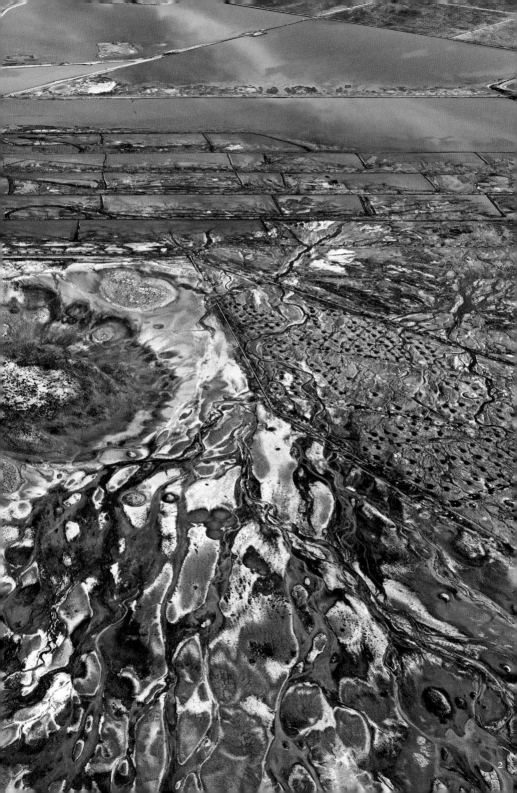

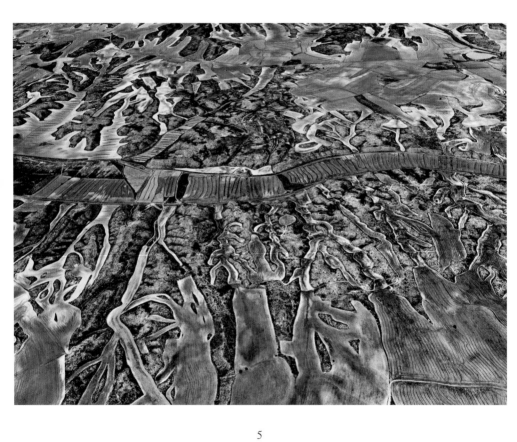

6

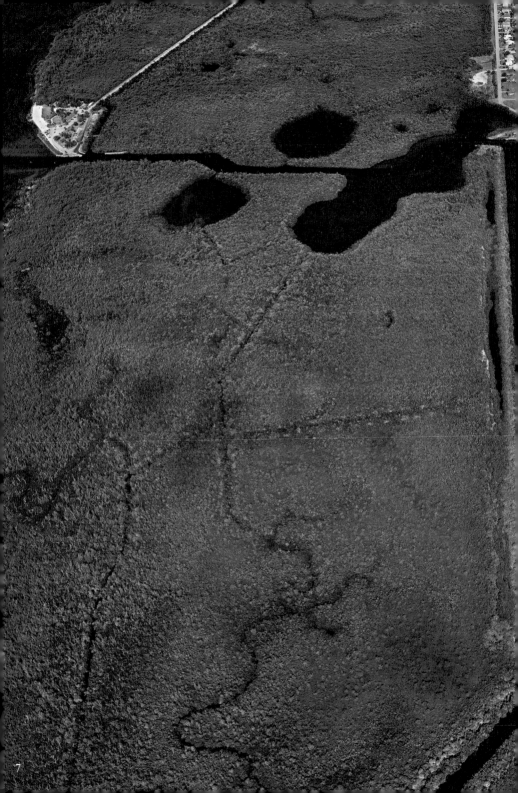

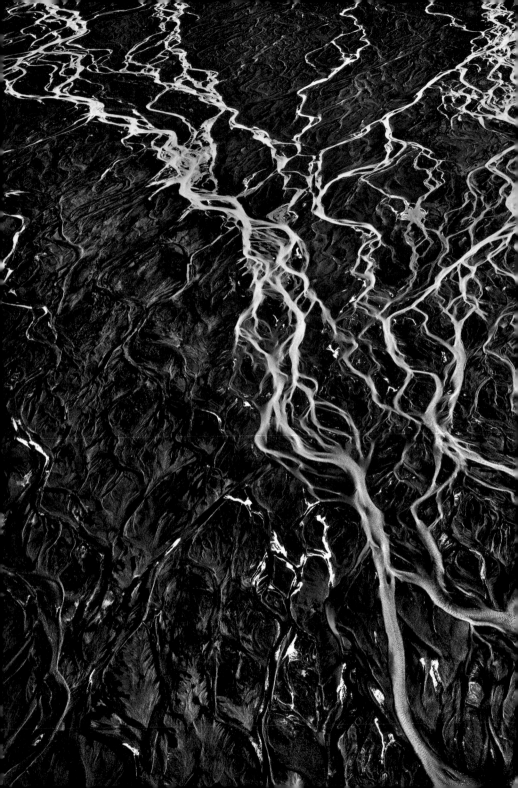

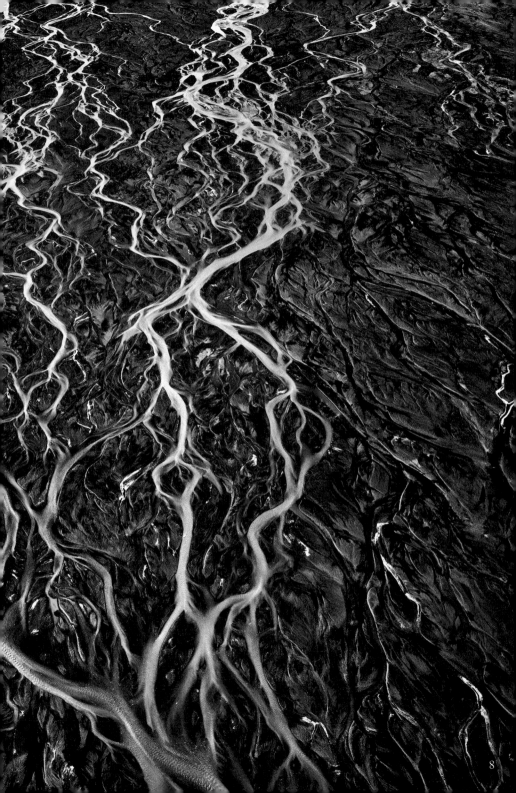

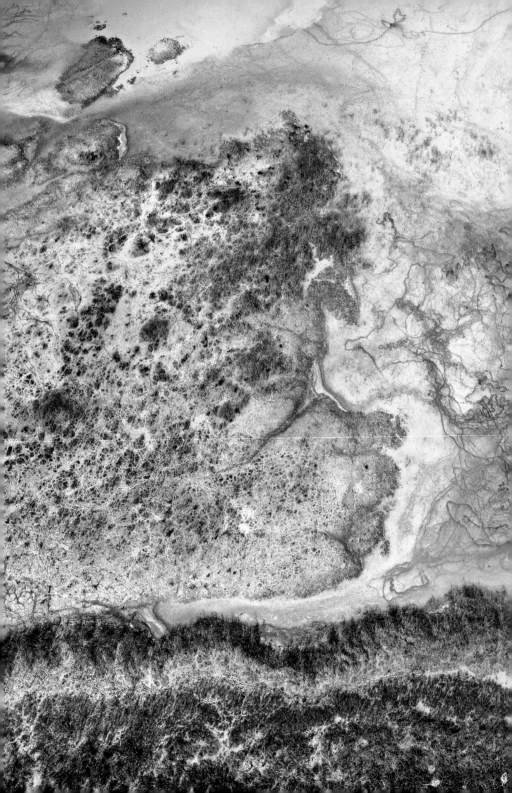

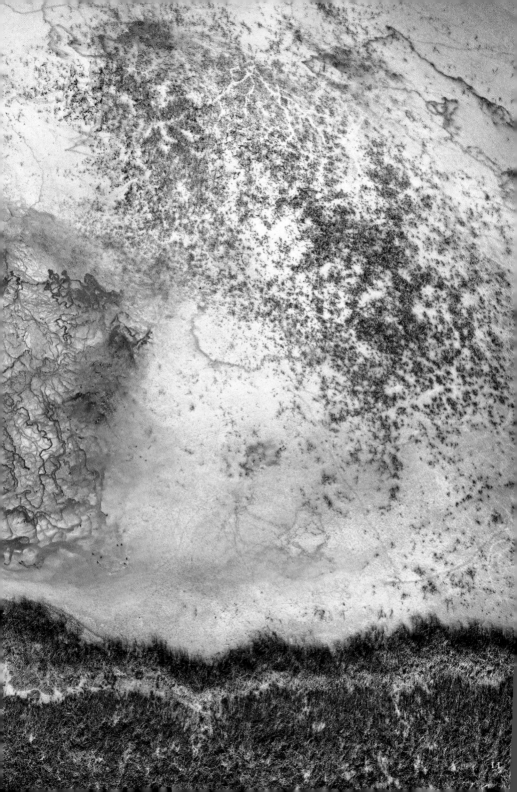

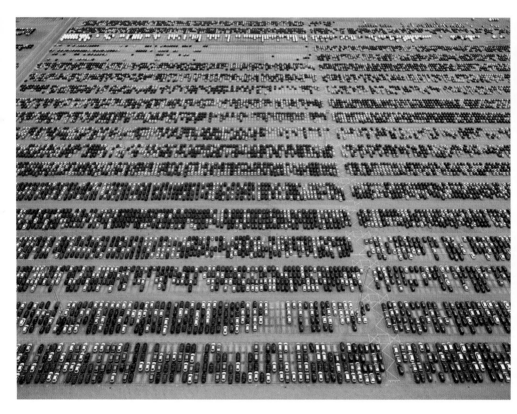

13

15

NEWS THAT MATTERS

www.groundup.org.za

Inside Taylors Buttons, London.
Courtesy of the author

THE LAST SHOPKEEPERS OF LONDON

David Flusfeder

E very few years, I buy a new pair of black jeans and I usually go to Trussons Menswear in Lower Marsh, Waterloo, to do so.

On my most recent visit, Barry, who is the fourth generation Trusson to run the shop, was sneezing. He'd had the flu jab a couple of days before and thought it had induced the onset of a fully fledged virus.

Trussons has been a gentlemen's outfitter for 151 years. The original, triple-fronted shop, across the road, was bombed in the war. The present one was converted from what had been the company's warehouse. Actually, 'present' is the wrong word, because by the time you read this, Trussons will be gone. A hotel is going up across the road and Barry didn't fancy sitting opposite a building site for the next couple of years.

'That's a shame,' I said.

I am going to miss Trussons. Barry's prices are good, and I like his stock, the Wrangler jeans and Gabicci jackets chosen (nowadays, one might say 'curated') by the reliable taste of someone who had been a mod in the 1960s. His sky-blue plastic carrier bags have the words MOD COMFYS printed on them. And Lower Marsh is one of those 'characterful' London streets, where the shops that have given it its character are being squeezed out by the rising costs of rents, leases and business rates.

Barry sniffed. He didn't share my concern. He owns the freehold and can make more money renting out the premises than he ever could operating his own establishment.

'I've had enough, to be honest,' he said.

The following morning, my new jeans somewhat outclassing my old footwear, I went to the Leonard Jay menswear shop on Southampton Row in Bloomsbury. There have often been sale signs in Leonard Jay's window. These ones read CLOSING DOWN, EVERYTHING MUST GO.

The lady on the ground floor called down to the owner, 'Mr Jay? Size eleven black leather Chelsea boot?'

I was invited downstairs, where Mr Jay, an energetic figure in tweed and corduroy and bright red running shoes, was finishing his breakfast. He didn't have elevens, but he did have ten and a half, which might be worth trying. He handed me the pair, asked me, as had the lady upstairs, whether I lived locally, and told me that he could easily get elevens if the ten and a halfs didn't fit. They slipped on without any need for the offered shoe horn.

'The best price anywhere,' he assured me, modestly.

Somehow I had also agreed to buy a pair of brown suede boots before we made our way back upstairs.

'How about a Harris tweed coat?'

Almost magically, I was now wearing a perfectly fitting overcoat that I would never have chosen for myself but which I wanted very much to own. Mr Jay must have noticed my concern as I looked down at the price tag.

'Don't worry about it, it won't be anything like that,' he said.

And nor was it. It was half that.

'A great price,' he said. 'Perhaps you'd be interested in a sports jacket?'

I managed to sidestep the jacket which he was advancing upon me with its sleeves open for my arms to fill. Instead, I paid for my new clothes, and his wife, the lady upstairs, gave me a kind of blessing.

'Wear them in good health,' she said.

Mr and Mrs Jay are actually called Lawrence and Tillie Jacobs. They've been working together in his shop for twenty-two years, since the last of their children left home. The closing-down signs in the windows, which I had taken as a sales ploy, were genuine and Leonard Jay of Bloomsbury really is going out of business.

'God made us a beautiful world and I want to see more of it. I'm out, I'm out, it's the end of an era. All the good salesmen are in Bushey.'

By which he meant the Jewish cemetery in Bushey, which is where my stepfather happens to be buried. His neighbours there may be the great London salesmen of the past, but Moris Dienstag wasn't one of them.

On Saturdays in the latter part of my teenage years, I worked at his shop, Everybody's Clothing Supply, Ltd. It sold new and second-hand men's clothing from the perpetually dismal spot it occupied near the Archway end of Holloway Road in north London. Moris had inherited the shop from his father, and was ineffectually running it slowly into the ground.

The boots I bought at Leonard Jay were just what I wanted, as was the overcoat, even if I hadn't known that I wanted it. Everything was expertly sized – in contrast to my stepfather, whose sizing tended to the narrow and pinched. This might have been an effect of the war he was always fighting with the Irish labourers, his core group of customers, who came in for clothes to wear on building sites. He referred to them, often in their hearing, as *schnorrers* and *time-wasters*. They in turn didn't hide their distaste for him, a dislike that ran uncomfortably close to anti-Semitism. The Irish invariably would argue that the jacket he had chosen for them was too small. 'Look,' they'd say, stretching their arms fully out in front of them, so that the bones of their wrists were visible from where the cuffs had ridden away.

'Do you walk around like that?' my stepfather would argue, sometimes then performing a gruesome mockery of a zombie with his own arms outstretched.

'It's too small,' they'd persist, getting angrier, and the situation would resolve in snappish bad temper on both sides and the customer walking out wearing a jacket that was two sizes too big.

This was my Saturday job; I felt like a prince in exile. I resented being there, resented the customers assuming I was his son (*'Step*son,' I'd instantly correct), and resented the stupidity of my stepfather, who had turned down the opportunity to buy the freehold from the landlord ('Why should I take on the aggravation?'). I'd dress myself in dead-men's suits and listen to the football reports on the radio and smoke thin roll-ups, because I wasn't being paid enough to afford proper cigarettes and in those days people thought nothing of walking into a clothes shop that smelled of tobacco.

The only time that I did pretend he was my actual father, I'd gone to buy a leather jacket from a shop in Camden Town where my stepfather assured me I could get a discount. He'd phoned ahead on my behalf.

'Young Everybody is here,' a shop assistant called out to the manager, a memory that still has the capacity to make me shiver.

I don't miss or mourn Everybody's Clothing Supply. No one else has. There is no history of it, no trace of it on the internet. But I was sorry to see Trussons and Leonard Jay go, and it became a kind of mission to find contemporaries of theirs that weren't closing down, establishments that have continued to flourish, or at least endure, shops that have been allowed to grow old.

The principle that guided me when choosing the places to visit, and proprietors to talk to and photograph, was that, like Trussons or Leonard Jay, they should have been in operation for at least fifty years, be a single concern, owned by a working proprietor. They should be the sorts of shops I was familiar with when I was young, where the customer enjoyed, or suffered, the personality of the owner while benefiting from their expertise. They should, in short, be idealised versions of the shop that I loathed beyond words as a boy.

Before I left Lawrence Jacobs's shop, we became diverted onto sporting events. His father had boxed; his uncle had been the boxing referee Mike Jacobs.

He pointed to one of the photographs above his till. 'That's me. I breed horses. Cheltenham. You've heard of that?'

'Yes. Of course.'

'And that's me. You know where that is?'

'Yes. Lords.'

'That's right.'

There was a relentless cheeriness about him, an enviable pleasure he took in his own sense of himself, the salesman's bullish energies, as he stood, ready to spring from the balls of his feet, to reach his next triumph.

He had had little choice about career. When he was at primary school, Lawrence Jacobs was diagnosed with severe asthma and sent away to a school in Broadstairs.

'We had no classes, just went for walks every day.' One of the results of this regimen was that when he returned home he failed his eleven-plus.

He became especially animated when I asked him about rivals and competitors. A salesman he knew, who worked for a wholesaler, had spent a couple of hours in Lawrence's shop, closely observing the operation, and then shortly afterwards opened his own shop, just down the road.

'I thought that was naughty, really naughty.'

It was an affront to the boxer's son. 'Whatever he sold, I'd put it in my window at a lower price.'

That's what you do with rivals. 'You see them off, I didn't have a choice.'

Lawrence Jacobs had no recollection of ever expecting or wanting to be anything other than a salesman. Before Maureen Rose married, she had wanted to be a florist. She now makes and sells buttons, and has done so for the last fifty-six years.

Throughout our conversation, Mrs Rose made buttons. Sitting on a stool behind the counter of Taylors Buttons, she would cut the measure of material, fold it, and insert it inside the press, which was a simple pair of moulds. The regular movements of squeezing the press and releasing the finished button were like breathing.

Her shop is on Cleveland Street in Fitzrovia. A blue plaque outside tells us that Charles Dickens twice lived here. There is little inside that would surprise him. The button press, which dates from the nineteenth century, came with the business that Maureen and her late husband Leon bought from Mr Taylor, the son of the original founder. Some of the buttons she sells are older still.

While we talked, a couple of young Japanese women came into the shop. They looked like fashion students who had found their way into a fairy tale. Taylors Buttons is, even more than you might expect, filled with buttons. There are buttons on every surface, including the floor. Hundreds upon hundreds of brown cardboard boxes, generally with a descriptive label and a colour and a sample button stuck to them, overfill the shelves that line every wall.

'I like the business. It's very mixed. It's a very old craft.'

Mrs Rose had just made 530 gold leather buttons. She provides buttons for haute couture, for bridal wear. She's made buttons for the royal family and was eligible for a royal warrant. She used to provide all Margaret Thatcher's buttons, a fact she volunteered as if she was expecting a warmer response than I was able to give. She does a lot of work for West End theatres and a note of mild disappointment entered her voice when she mentioned, not quite complaining, that none of her theatrical customers ever invites her to their shows.

The Japanese women reached for boxes and timidly looked over to Mrs Rose for permission to go through them, which she benevolently gave. Every so often they would share a delighted discovery with each other and then hold up a button to the proprietor to ask how much it cost. 'Ninety-nine pee,' Mrs Rose said, and repeated the sum, and then helpfully sorted through the change on the outstretched palm to take the correct amount. 'That one? That's much more expensive. That's very old. One pound seventy-five.'

And then we resumed talking. 'It's very penny ante, you're never going to make a fortune.' She makes enough of a living to satisfy herself, to pay the rent and the wages of the shop assistant she employs for those days she doesn't work. At least once a year, a collector visits from America to stock up on treasures which she locks away in drawers back home. Maureen Rose was slightly puzzled that the collector didn't put them on display, but her manner, of gentle amused courtesy, remained unchanged. Her long-time rival, The Button Queen, whose high prices she marvelled at, has recently closed its London shop.

She has a son who works in IT, and this, I found, was going to be a recurring theme – the lack of interest in the family business from the next generation. Her son designed her website, as did Barry Trusson's son for his father. Only Adam Graham, son of the owner of William Gee, had taken the next step towards the company rather than away from it.

William Gee has been in existence for 111 years, consolidated by a merger in 1963 of the previously competing haberdashery companies owned by the Gee and Graham families. It's on Kingsland Road in Dalston, in east London, next door to an abandoned shop on one side and a large Oxfam on the other. (This is the familiar sight of the modern British high street. The proliferation of charity shops is a result of their exemption from at least 80 per cent of business rates, often rising to 100 per cent.) William Gee's own unloved exterior seems to indicate that it belongs to the Dalston of industrial and economic decline of a generation ago, when, as the owner Jeffrey Graham says, 'no one wanted to piss in that direction' – but appearances deceive: William Gee was the busiest of the shops I visited, as well as the one with the clearest and boldest plans for the future.

The business used to be primarily a wholesaler, selling cloth and zips and linings and sewing threads to department stores and high street shops. It had a workforce of more than sixty people and even used to produce its own buttons. Jeffrey Graham had a Saturday job here in the late 1960s, but had no intention of joining the firm.

The first of his family to go to university, he studied politics and sociology. He'd inhaled the spirit of 1968, the Paris demonstrations, philosophies of liberation. He became a teacher and emigrated to Israel, where he lived on a kibbutz that was run in the old-fashioned socialist collectivist spirit.

He became the principal of a secondary school, but returned to London in 1988 with his wife and four children in response to the decline of the kibbutz movement and the rightward shift within Israeli politics.

Things had changed here too, and William Gee along with it. The company, which had always run a shop for the local community, was moving away from being a wholesaler.

'There was a big change in fashion in the 1990s. Clothing manufacturers were sourcing from abroad, Eastern Europe, then Africa, then China, wherever labour was cheapest. The factories closed down in Dalston, and the fashion designers moved in.

'I'd never quite understood the concept of transferable skills before, but all the things I'd learned as a high school principal equipped me to do this job.'

Jeffrey Graham talks in clear, measured sentences, with precision and humour. He has the good teacher's knack of conveying information in what feels like a conversation rather than a lecture.

We were talking in his office behind the main shop. His son was in another office working on the website and online shop. While I'd waited to see Jeffrey, a non-virtual customer, slightly nervously referring to a sewing pattern on her phone, had been patiently helped by the shop assistant.

'I should be using a curved thread, right?'

'Actually, a straight thread would probably be better.'

The next customer had more confidently asked for what she needed and then broke off to say, 'I haven't seen you recently.' The shop assistant told her that she was recently back from maternity leave.

'When people come into shops,' Jeffrey said, 'they're often

soulless places. But traditional places, you go in, strike up a chat, and you come back. And there's been a massive increase in fashion departments, in schools as well as in art colleges. Teachers, students, graduates, interns. I tell the staff, "Treat everyone as if they're the new Alexander McQueen."

'Another big thing: a lot of sewing schools have set up, particularly in this area. Since the financial crash ten years ago, making things, repairing things – we can work in coordination with the local sewing schools, in Broadway Market, hold workshops with them.'

I remarked that the company's website and online shop, which was set up by Adam, is very impressive.

'The successful businesses today are the ones that combine the bricks-and-mortar element with the digital experience. John Lewis has done it brilliantly. Marks & Spencer hasn't. BHS didn't. The other side is, how efficient is the bricks and mortar? My bane is when customers say, "I didn't know you did that." It's our fault for not putting it out there. The shop has to be a more interactive space, not just selling a box of sewing threads.'

As war-damaged Trussons did in the 1940s, Jeffrey Graham is planning on relocating the shop to the warehouse they own on the other side of Kingsland Road. There he will present his vision of the 'interactive space'. The existing premises will be developed commercially and residentially.

The heart sinks slightly. Dalston is the exemplification of that now familiar gentrification pattern in which artists and studios and, indeed, the next Alexander McQueens serve as a kind of wedge for the ensuing movement of money. This is what the avant-garde has become, an advance force for property developers and estate agents.

I asked him if the red flag still flies somewhere in his heart. 'Well, pinkish,' he said.

Sharp's Fishing Tackle has no website, or staff. Bob Sharp inherited his business, and the freehold, and his love of fishing, from his father. Like Jeffrey Graham, Sharp had his own career before going into the family business. He was a soldier for three years and then a British Telecom engineer for thirty-three, the last ten of those as a manager which he combined with running the shop. 'Most BT engineers had two jobs. Just shut your mouth, get your job done, and nobody will bother you.'

Sharp's Fishing Tackle is filled with boxes and plastic cases of anglers' supplies. There's a very narrow space between the counter and the higgledy-piggledy stacks of boxes of marine pellets where the visitor's chair goes. 'People say, why don't you get rid of these boxes and I say, why don't you go away?'

Sharp grew up in this area, which is on a hill that descends into Kentish Town and rises towards Belsize Park. Nearby is a church and an undertakers. 'There used to be a post office and an oil shop, a little hardware store, all the different kinds of trades.' The premises now are all being bought up by developers to convert into flats.

'A Chinese group wanted to buy. They sent a lawyer to see me. "I'll make you an offer you can't refuse." I showed him where the door is.'

Bob was full of patter, spiky little jokes and quips and homilies. 'You've got to think like a fish . . . not drink like one.' But then the stories grew, in detail and scope, and I became the happy recipient of Bob Sharp's anecdotes and histories.

He's pushing eighty, but he's in great shape: short, a little wider than when he was a rifleman in North Africa, long white hair pulled back in a ponytail. The rhythms of this life are congenial ones. He lives above the shop, opens up when he feels like it. Other days he's just as likely to be fishing.

'What kind of fishing?'

'Every kind. Coarse, game, commercial, river, canal, sea, lake, beach . . . you get the idea?'

I've never fished, and now I wanted to, hearing Bob describe the serenity it brings, the heightened awareness of one's own skills and capacities, as well as enhanced knowledge and understanding of the world.

I had my standard set of questions for the shopkeepers. With Bob Sharp I didn't get through them all. I was too busy listening. An army story that began with a basket of stolen figs ended in him witnessing the death of an unpopular soldier, shot as if by accident on manoeuvres ('happens all the time in the army'). He told me how he had 'midwifed three of my four children', and I listened to episodes from his father's life, his shrewdness, his occasional roguery, Bob's utter respect for him, and the moment when Bob had to switch off his father's life-support machine in hospital.

Bob sold his first handmade, self-designed flies when he was ten, crafting them from matchsticks and sofa-cushion feathers ('hen and cock feathers are different'). He sold them to local fishermen. His customers are different now, 'a lot of Russians and East Europeans'.

The door rattled in the doorway, and a funeral procession went past – plumed horses pulling the hearse, four black limousines following – and the landline happened to ring with its antique bell that was once so familiar, and now feels like something from a stage or film set, but there was nothing artful or ironic about it. It was just a telephone ringing in the shop of the former telecom engineer, an old machine that worked and hadn't been replaced, because there was no need to do so, and Bob went to answer it without excuse or apology. ∎

Chelsey Minnis

Darling

Oh, it's you.
I never could resist anything that belonged to someone else.
I suppose you feel the same.
That's a very promising black eye.
If you want one, fix it yourself.

You wear a big, gold belt buckle with your name on it.
Now, I really like your eyes when they look at me with that look.
The one that is so fair-minded.
It's dangerous like a very powerful doorbell.
Or a portrait covered with a blanket.

You didn't lock your door.
You never were very particular about your associations.
Does it give you a lovely guilty feeling?
To me you're a national disgrace.
Please act accordingly.

I didn't hit you very hard.
It all depends what you want out of life.
Never mind talking.
I know I'm a bad woman.
I think you'll find it to our mutual benefit.

Sure, I'm decent.
I'll have to try that sometime.
Don't shout, darling. I'm not used to it.
I need my hand back now.
When I don't like something, I give it back.

You find it amusing to tempt me?
How right you are.
The word is 'incautious' and I am.
You might be bluffing, but I'm not.
You wouldn't happen to have any extra pajamas?

Don't play cards with me, darling, I'm a cheat.
It's true. I'm weak.
I'd like to take a bite out of you.
How about your wife? Is she broad-minded all of a sudden?
If you're going to leave, then why don't you hurry?

THE PERSEIDS

Susan Straight

D ante could hear the small truck laboring up the slight grade of
Baseline Avenue. He heard the clattering as it turned onto the
long dirt-covered road leading north toward his street. He recognized
the shitty engine and the cargo in the bed. Meth heads. They'd come
past his house last night, checking out the cell towers at the short dead
end of Minerva Court.

He hadn't thought they'd come back so fast. It was 2 a.m. No
other vehicles around, just the long whine and then the downshift
of semi-trucks heading down the Cajon Pass into San Bernardino,
coming from Vegas. When he was little, listening in bed, he imagined
the trucks like dinosaurs farting their way down the grade.

Tonight was supposed to be better than last night for the show of
stars, so Dante had settled down after midnight wearing his hoodie,
holding the binoculars. Utter darkness wasn't possible, but he left
his phone inside so even that blue light wouldn't show. Behind the
house were only black acres of sandy field and the old corral. Then
the arroyo and the freeway.

He turned the binoculars on his house – thirty feet away down
the long cement path bordered with river rock, past the old plow and
stone water trough. The ancient redwood shingles on the house had
darkened to tight black scales. The first time his best friend Manny's

father picked up Dante for baseball practice, he said to Dante's father, 'Damn – these shingles aren't even painted, homes!'

Dante's father said, 'Linseed oil and turpentine. 1889. Sinks in permanent.'

'I already had to repaint my stucco, man, after a year.'

'You got a new house,' his father had laughed. 'Me – I relax. Watch *Saturday Night Fever. Wizard of Oz.* Whatever my wife wants to see.'

Manny Jr waited until they were hitting grounders to say, 'Your dad watches some weird shit. My dad just watches sports.'

Dante said, 'He met my mom when they were freshmen in theater class. He built a whole graveyard on stage just so he could watch her sing.'

His father's name was Grief, after some guy who came out from Mississippi with his father's great-grandmother, Lily. His mother's name was Larette, after her grandmother back in Louisiana. Larette had painted the two pillars of river rock holding up the porch roof. Fat white pearls in the dark. The front window's original glass was all wavery – like black Saran Wrap. Dante's phone was filed in his mother's coupon box: under P, with Procter & Gamble. He missed her so much he looked at the coupons every day, even though that was babyish.

Strange to have no white moths or the golden beetles his mother used to call candlebeasts. Because there were no streetlights anymore. The copper wiring had been stolen from all of them six months ago. Dante's father had put up a solar porch light, but Dante had covered it tonight, even though his father never wanted it completely dark. 'There's only us left on the block,' his father said. 'My grandpa said Lily used to talk about how one fire tamed the wild. We got one light bulb here.'

Lily came out to San Bernardino with the Mormons in their wagons. Not because she wanted to. They had campfires and kerosene lanterns. The same stars shooting across the sky as right now, and Lily had been up listening for horse thieves. Cattle rustlers. She was out here in absolute darkness.

Now it was the Wild Wild West again. These two guys in the raggedy white Ford Ranger were copper rustlers. Dante heard the engine wheezing around the corner, sounding like asthmatic Manny on his way to third base. The truck came slow down Minerva Court, headlights off. If only they wanted to make sure the stars were bright. But they were hunting.

Dante had seen their truck bed last night. Torn-off freeway guardrails stacked like dirty gray rib bones. Brass fittings from irrigation systems, poking up like beaked bird heads. They'd driven on the soft sand at the edges of the narrow asphalt road, all the way into the bushes that hid the fence around the cell tower substation. They'd gotten out, tools clanking.

'No room tonight, dude,' the taller man had said. 'Not for that much wire.' They got back in the truck and reversed, lights off, all the way down the road.

'Fake-ass palm trees,' his father had said about the three cell towers they'd been eyeing back in January. 'How you gonna put up something so expensive and advertise it to thieves?'

How big was a catalytic converter? Manny's father and Tyrone had both been pissed off last week because someone stole the catalytic converters off seven trucks, right in the driveways of their houses. Guys went out in the morning for work and their trucks wouldn't start. They lived up in Oak Creek Ranch. The creek was covered over with cement and hollow fake boulders, but ducks still hung out there. Short steep white driveways like pull tabs in front of each house.

His father laughed at Manny Sr. 'You got a two-car garage! Why wasn't your truck in there?'

Manny Sr said, 'Already got it full of stuff, homes.'

Every day, Dante's father parked his truck on the sandy shoulder of Minerva Court, and in summer, Dante sat in the bed to watch the sky. He told Manny and Montrell they could race tumbleweeds out here. Saddle 'em up and bet on 'em, they were so big.

'Tumbleweeds are the edelweiss of our cul-de-sac,' his mother used to joke, last year.

'Mormons didn't speak German or French,' his father used to say.
'Cul-de-sac. Like *culo*. Spanish for ass. We're at the ass end of the
road and the city doesn't give a damn the streetlights have been out
for months,' his father had told Montrell last week.

August. The time of the Perseids never varied. That was why
Dante's mother had taught him the stars. Must be ninety degrees even
now, at 2 a.m. Hundred and twelve today. No coyotes. No rabbits.
Nothing moved but the Ranger, creeping toward the cell towers.

They must have come back to strip them out. Shit. Dante didn't
want to go inside. They weren't predators. They were vermin.
Scavengers. They'd be fast. It was so dark they'd never notice him.
And he didn't want to miss the meteors.

He lowered his upper body down onto the metal grooves of his
father's truck bed, between the two toolboxes bolted in on each side.
Now he could see only what he'd come out here to see: the sky.

'Right here,' Dante's father had told him when he was seven, his
arm sweeping the horizon of the San Bernardino Mountains,
the Cajon Pass, the sandy flats and eucalyptus windbreaks and deep
arroyos, the tumbleweeds blue-green and big as hippos rising from
the earth, 'here you have predators and vermin and scavengers.
Your mom doesn't want me scaring you. But that's my job. Right
here, you got scorpions, tarantulas, black widows, brown recluse
and centipedes. So watch the woodpile and the fences. You got
rattlesnakes, especially out by the windmill. They hung out back there
when I was little.' He pointed to the arroyo. 'You got coyotes, bobcats,
feral dogs. Raccoons will fight you. Over by Colton, they have wild
burros. Kick the shit out of you. Bite you with them big burro teeth.
When your Uncle Perry got the deputy job, he got bit by a damn
burro and I had to go help him out.'

Then his father had pointed to the freeway, and the edge of LA.
Green city trees and billboards in the distance. 'You got two kinds of
humans might come up on you. Assholes and knuckleheads. Assholes
want to hurt you. Not eat you – just hurt you. Knuckleheads are just

stupid. You gotta learn to tell the difference fast.'

Now the truck was idling in front of the cell towers. The men were probably thinking that the house and the truck Dante was in were abandoned.

Assholes or knuckleheads – he couldn't tell yet. A thread of cigarette smoke hung in the air. One guy said, 'Don't fuck up, Carlos. Pull the wire. I'll be back. I'm getting that marker off the old sign we passed.'

The historic marker on Baseline. The brass plaque. The Mormons.

Carlos said, 'Too fuckin' boring with no radio. We should play some Metallica, man. Exit light. Enter night.'

'Shut up, Carlos.' The taller man reversed and went back down the street, so slowly Dante could hear rocks pop softly off the bald treads. Dante pulled the binoculars onto his chest under the black sweatshirt. He kept his eyes closed. Mouth closed. No white.

The one who climbed the pole to the vault was Carlos. The three fake palm trees and four real ones inside the chain-link fence were topped with barbed wire.

He still had one message from his mother on his phone: 'Dante, sweetie, I'll be late from work. Mrs Batiste is really sick now, and we took her to St Bernardine's. Bring the Sunday paper inside so the rain doesn't get it.' Dante hadn't heard the ring, watching basketball on TV, his headphones on. That was back in December, about a week before his mother was admitted to St Bernardine's herself.

She never came home. There was a photo of her on the fireplace next to the coupon box. Four nurses on graduation day, all friends from college. Cynthia and Saqqara came from LA for his mother's funeral. Merry Jordan, the other nurse, had killed herself after her son got shot by a cop. Dante's mother had stayed in her bedroom for two days after that, and when she came out to the kitchen, the edges of her hair were cloudy around her forehead from tears and sweat and her face in the pillow.

The Sunday paper had her coupons. Hundreds of them arranged alphabetically in the wooden box that once held Lily's sewing supplies. The coupons killed him. A few times after she got sick, she cried because some of her favorite coupons were expiring and she couldn't get to the store. 'Grief!' she cried. 'You forgot Tide and Charmin!'

His father had given her the cedar box, flowers and garlands carved along the top, when they got married. Lily's husband had made it, back in Mississippi, before Lily was sold to the Mormons.

Carlos was working on the fence. Dante could hear bolt cutters pinging on each diamond of chain link, and then a sweeter, more silvery ping on the strands of barbed wire. Pliers and wire cutters and a hammer clanking on Carlos's belt as he approached the pole.

If Carlos glanced down into the truck bed when he made it to the top, he'd only see a heap of clothes. Black work clothes. His father's 1958 Apache was too old to have a catalytic converter. Dante could be cool. He heard the thud of each boot on the rungs of the tower.

'Who the hell designed those fake trees?' Manny Sr said one day. 'Must have been some dude from back East. No coconuts out here! Dates, man. Little gold dates.'

'An unfortunate mix,' his father said. 'Those panels look like flat green bananas.'

His father's favorite word was unfortunate. When Dante struck out at the baseball diamond his father would say, 'No fortune for you, man, not tonight.'

Manny's mom always brought snacks – KFC popcorn nuggets. She'd say to Dante's mother, 'New eyeshadow, no?'

'An unfortunate selection,' his father said.

'I had a coupon for Revlon,' his mother said. 'Magnificent Metallics. Two for ninety-nine cents.'

Dante looked at his mother's eyelids. Not gold – kind of dull yellow, like bee pollen.

'Looks like eight days after the fight,' his father joked.

Manny's mother said, 'You never get mad at him, Larette? *Fortunado.*'

'You both work with death all the time, man, and you're always happy,' Manny's father said, holding out the chicken for the boys.

'I'm not dead,' Dante's mother said. 'So I'm always happy.'

'My clients don't always end up dead. Not every time,' Dante's father said. 'And someday Dante'll hit a homer.'

'You work with death all day too, Mami,' Manny said. 'The chickens are hella dead when you fry 'em.'

Manny's mother sighed. She was the manager at the KFC.

'Grief!' his father's friend Tyrone shouted as he walked up. He still had his EMT uniform on. 'You ain't sang yet? Larette ain't made you sing tonight?'

Larette was so pretty that after Grief had built every set for their high school productions, he followed her to San Bernardino Valley College, where he built sets for all their shows, too. Larette tested him on the lyrics to each song she sang, in every musical. *Carmen Jones. The Wiz. Grease. Spamalot.*

But to torture him in front of Tyrone or Manny's parents or his uncle, she always picked *The Sound of Music*. It was just familiar enough that they'd all recognize something to laugh at. Grief was required to sing two answering verses of whatever Larette chose, and everyone would fall out laughing on the bleachers when he did.

That night, his mother wanted payback for his comment about the eyeshadow. She smiled sweetly and sang her favorite eleven notes. The eleven notes of 'My Favourite Things'. 'Pieces of chicken all coated in batter . . .'

Grief rolled his eyes. 'My son will hit a home run with a big . . . clatter?'

She shook her head. 'That was terrible.'

Six months ago, during the first Santa Ana wind after she died, Dante had watched the cell towers. North of Baseline, the wind was so strong that even the metal fronds moved a little, like they were dignified and reserved – superior in their stiffness to the wild tossing and crashing of the real fronds. Tumbleweeds flew out of the corral, carried so high that two were caught in the fake trees and hung there for weeks, like giant Christmas ornaments.

That night, his father had sat by the window with him, and sung her second-favorite tune as tenderly as the hatchet-faced Captain von Trapp: 'Edelweiss'. 'Tumbleweed, tumbleweed, every winter you beat me. Big and brown, thorns and round, you will always defeat me.'

C arlos had made it to the top. Tools banging. The Ranger was laboring back toward Baseline Avenue. Baseline and Meridian. The beginning of southern California, where they laid out the streets that went all the way to LA and Hollywood and Santa Monica. The closest house was a mile west – Uncle Perry's. Dante used to have to walk to Uncle Perry's before school if his mother had to stay with someone who'd died, waiting for the coroner. If Dante complained, his father would say, 'Lily walked seven hundred miles. That was a hella walk, so stop bellyachin'. What my grampa used to say. Bellyachin'.'

The Ranger droned like a pissed-off wasp in the distance, then stopped. Chisel or hammer. Speed freaks took everything. Last summer they took the bleachers from the park. Every single piece of aluminum. They took the copper wire from the park lights. No more games.

Jonny Frias said, 'Who buys bleachers and melts them down? Who doesn't call the cops when some *pendejo* shows up to sell bleachers?'

'Like the Walking Dead,' Tyrone said. 'They come out at night. Season's over now, fellas. Park ain't got no money to replace the lights.'

Dante breathed shallow now, wishing this dude Carlos would hurry up. The meteors peaked between 2 and 3 a.m. He'd been waiting all summer.

A screech of metal being pried open, like a crazy jay. A mockingbird started up for a minute, then stopped abruptly. Carlos must have awakened it. Mockingbirds didn't song-fight in August. They fought in spring. Starting near midnight, lasting until dawn, the birds delirious and high, repeating the same notes over and over from the two tall palms with shaggy fronds perfect for nests.

'The trees are alive with the sound of mur-der,' his mother would sing, and then glance at his father, waiting. 'Ah-ah-ah-ahh.'

'The mockingbird sings to keep other asshole birds far away,' his father would sing. 'Ah-ah-ah-ahhhh,' he'd add.

His mother tested his father frequently, randomly. He had to come up with something quick or she'd talk yang for the whole night.

'The hills are alive with the sound of killing,' she sang.

'The coyote laughs he got a Si-a-mese today – aah-aah-ah-ah.'

Fucking Carlos. Fucking bird. Tears slid sideways into Dante's ears. Shit. Shiny on his face. Like torture not to wipe them away. If he moved, Carlos might hear him.

When Carlos pulled the wires, everything would blink and turn black. The only other houses on Minerva Court were boarded up now. Mrs Jameson and Mrs Batiste had both died last year, and their sons were in Rialto and LA. No one wanted to live way out here.

The explosion was as loud as fireworks but more personal. Contained somehow. Damp and muffled for one second, and then – boom.

Dante opened his eyes. The shower of sparks splayed out like a huge Roman candle attached to the pole – a burst of light curving, floating, then invisible.

Carlos sailed out from the metal tower like he was not human. A bulk of cloth heavy and soft. An echoless medium-sized sound on the asphalt. A swift nothing.

Silence. Carlos made no sound.

He was burnt. Maybe that had made his body instantly softer. Rendered. Dante felt vomit rising in his belly. We rendered the beef fat into tallow for candles. Biddy and Hannah and I walked seven hours behind the wagon today. Elder Amasa wanted candles. From Lily's journal.

Then came soft sounds. About four feet away – Carlos had flown north, toward the Apache. Hissing – breathing, or the skin, or something else? Dante was afraid to look. The smell was so strong and sweet and terrible that he pushed the strings of his hoodie into his mouth and sucked hard to keep from throwing up. One last whisper.

Close by. An exhalation. The strings tasted of Tide. Don't cry. Don't.

Then the silence was complete. The three swamp coolers attached to the windows of the living room, his father's bedroom and his own room all went quiet, as if stunned. The house would be an oven in about ten minutes. Unbearable. Fifteen at the most.

Dante had ten minutes, then, until his father woke up and realized the swamp cooler had stopped. Maybe fifteen. He'd come outside to check them.

The darkness was complete. At the sound of the explosion the Ranger had snarled to life and headed back this way. Dante slid his feet out from under the folded tarp. He got out the cop flashlight Uncle Perry had given him years ago. Four-battery, he called it. Dante had a couple minutes before the Ranger made it back.

Dante crouched by the tailgate and turned on the flashlight, training it on the dark heap. A human burnt to lava. Black and red. Black shiny as obsidian through the holes in the jacket. Blacker than any skin. Red, not shiny. Red like the posters in biology class. The back of his head red. The sheath of muscle over his skull exposed. No glisten. Smoked.

Dante dropped the flashlight onto the ground and threw up over the tailgate, holding tight to the rough paint. Cap'n Crunch he'd eaten at midnight. Quivering puddle next to the black boots. Saliva dripped from his mouth and he threw up again, heaving and heaving.

The swamp coolers dripped condensation onto the sand around the house.

The freeway lights to the east were still shining. Semi trucks still shifting gears. But honking horns out on Baseline, which was never free of cars. People who hated the freeway would drive to Rialto or Ontario or Pomona the old way, even at 2 a.m. If the signals were out, someone was gonna die. Someone else besides Carlos.

He put his leg up over the tailgate and just then a tiny breeze sent the smell into his face. He threw up green liquid onto the old chrome bumper. Dizzy and fire behind his eyelids. The Ranger screeched around the corner fast, onto his street. Dante lay back down, shaking, pulling the hood up, swallowing the acid scouring his throat.

'Sing. Sing.' What his mother had whispered to his father. What Dante did inside his head when gangsters came up on him and Manny and Montrell at the mall, shoving them around. What he did when they stood at the coffin.

Raindrops on roses and whiskers on kittens. Clorox and Dove Bars and hell no on mittens.

His mother sang with all the old people in hospice. 'I take care of them until they pass,' she told him when he was eight, scared of the word. Not hospital. Hospice. He was afraid cancer was contagious. He wouldn't get up on her lap when she wore the apricot-colored scrubs. Everyone had cancer. It must seep into her cheeks and fingers and wrists. He ran from her, but his father caught him and made him kiss her. When he was ten, she told him the words. Carcinogen. Metastasize. 'It can't jump out of someone's mouth onto me, baby.'

The smell of Carlos had jumped into his mouth. He heaved again and threw up bile under the toolbox. The Ranger pulled into the oleander bushes. Shit. Carlos. The name was already imprinted in his brain. Under the muscles of his scalp.

Bacterial pneumonia had jumped out of Mrs Batiste's mouth into Larette's. She had lasted two weeks. Thought she had a cold. His father took her to St Bernardine's – the tall buildings to the east. Their lights always on. His father always looked in that direction before he left for work.

'Fuck. Fuck. Fuck. Fuck.' The guy in the Ranger did not speak loudly, but it was a distinct word that carried in the silence. He got out of the car and walked toward Carlos. So tall Dante could see the upper half of him. He heard a knee joint crack. The flashlight click. Asshole or knucklehead. Drunk or high or an idiot. 'Fuck,' he said one more time.

A sigh. A sigh from the asphalt. Was that a breath? Or the skin releasing a breath?

What if Carlos was alive inside that crust of black skin? Dante shivered, clenched his jaw shut.

The tall guy said it again. 'Fuck.' Then he started walking back toward the Ranger.

He was leaving Carlos. No. Hell no. A dead body right here by his father's truck? Dante calling the cops, and when they came, it'd be Dante by a dead dude? Hell no.

Dante raised up, got on his knees and said, 'You finna pack him up, right?'

The man turned and shone the flashlight on Dante. He pulled a gun from his waistband with the other hand and walked back toward Dante, holding both up like movie six-shooters. Black shiny forehead over a black bandanna. 'The fuck did you say?' Wiry white dude voice.

'Sing at death,' his mother had said. Shoot me then. The cab window hot at his back. 'Fin-na pack-him-up,' he said clearly. 'Your friend.'

'Speak English, bro. You saw what happened?' The ears were pink. The fingers around the gun. The black was paint. Like in football. Damn – this was a white guy.

'How I'm not gon' see that and he fell right here?'

'What the fuck are you doin' out here? At fuckin' 2 a.m?'

'Perseids, man.'

'I told you to speak English. Bro.' He waved the gun.

'Stars.' No. I'm not telling you. I am not your bro. Brah. His mother used to say after a stranger got happy, 'I am not your girl, and I am not planning to go anywhere.' The gun. Barrel like one nostril of the bull Uncle Perry once kept in the corral. Bull named Coalmine.

'Stand up. Hands up, too. I will fuckin' shoot you. Why are you out here?'

Dante stood. His hood fell. He lifted his hands. Distinctly. Each word careful. 'Meteors. Shooting stars. Tonight.'

'Are you messing with me? Don't mess with me right now. You got a fuckin' piece? Hand it out here. Slow.'

'No gun.' Dante lifted his hands higher.

Definitely a speed freak. Not a knucklehead. Talking too fast. Not looking down. His truck engine clicked and clicked. Overhot. The swamp coolers on Dante's house ticked and dripped. If his father came out now, the asshole would shoot his father, too.

Then a breeze came and wafted the smell straight toward them. The asshole dropped to one knee and dropped the flashlight. He pulled the bandanna down, gasping, his face cleaved in half. White lips open like a fish. He rested the hand with the gun on his thigh.

The hot wind picked up and rustled the oleander. 'Whose truck is this? You're not old enough to drive.' The man waited. 'What are you doing out here?'

'I live here.'

'Who the fuck still lives out here?' The guy didn't take his eyes off Dante's face. 'This is Mormonland.'

Congratulations – he'd read the historical marker before he stole it. The heat was building inside the house. Coolers tick, ticking. No power. Dante said, 'My dad's people came out with the Mormons.'

'Bullshit. Ain't no black Mormons. You're out here in a hoodie.' He waved the gun toward the house, like an idiot. Like the pistol was an extension of his finger. 'Your gangbanger friends in there?'

Dante thought of Carlos's last breath. He took a smaller sip of air and closed his lips. Don't hurl. The asshole might get startled and shoot you. Asshole in blackface. He went black to blend with the dark, or he wanted the cops to look for a brother if someone reported the theft.

'Who lives there?'

'Me and my dad.'

'Where's your dad?'

'At work.'

'He left you alone?'

'He works night security at the construction site by the freeway. Somebody stole the crane last month. On the flatbed. The county hired my dad.' Before he could help it, he recalled Manny Sr saying, 'Who buys a crane?'

'Where's your mom?'

Dante said, 'None of your damn business.'

And the guy murmured as if to himself, 'Yeah, who the fuck wants to live out here?'

Dante's eyes stung. 'I'm thirteen. Legal to be home.'

The man spoke casually again, as if still talking to himself. 'Your house doesn't even look black.'

Dante looked up at the sky. Perseids. Hundreds of scribbles of silver. Less than a second to linger. Dissipate. Ash.

Then he said, 'Really? The wood is black.'

The guy turned the gun back on him. 'Fuck you. It looks like a cowboy house.'

'Actually it is.' How long was meth head attention span? Would he just shoot when he got bored? Fuck it. 'What should be out in the yard, man?' Dante said. 'Watermelons? Statue of Eazy-E?'

The guy rubbed his hand across his mouth and looked toward the Cajon Pass. He wanted to be on the freeway now. The bandanna hung around his neck like he was a fake train robber. Speed scabs like black sowbugs on his jaw. When he squinted, his front teeth showed, big and creamy and square like Rice Chex.

'Finna? What the fuck is that?'

This dude was so high. 'Finna. We finna go to the store.'

'Pick him up. Get out and pick him up. You finna whatever the fuck it is.'

'Hell no.'

'I'll shoot your black ass,' he said, and lifted the gun to Dante's face.

It had to be so hot inside the house by now. No cooler by the bed. No clock radio playing quiet storm. Old-school R&B love songs to mask the singing coyotes and mockingbirds that made his father cry. The hills and trees alive with the sound of music. Sweat dripping into his dad's eyes even if they were closed. Salt. Stinging.

'Pick him up.' The man took two more steps toward Dante.

'Time for you to hat up, man,' Dante said, staring straight into the nostril of the gun. He waited for his father. He spoke his father's language. Man, your friend Montrell needs to hat up right now because I'm tired of feedin' his crumb-snatcher ass. Even with coupons, right, Larette? How can y'all eat so much cereal she gotta file 'em under General Mills? The whole corporation! His mother so mad at herself, the week before she died. Twelve coupons expired. Good ones. Tide and Pantene and General Mills. All that Cap'n Crunch. The vomit already drying into a yellow cow patty next to Carlos's boots.

Dante propped his hands on the tailgate and closed his eyes. He swung his legs over, as he had hundreds of times when his father delivered him to the ballpark, and he waited for the sound. For the bullet in his spine. The smell. The soft sand under his Jordans. The same sand where Lily's horses stood while they drank at the old trough.

Dante closed his eyes. He bent and touched Carlos's boots. He put his fingers around the black heels.

'Turn him over. You're a weird fuckin' kid. You shouldn't be sittin' outside. You should be watchin' TV in your fuckin' house like a normal kid.'

Dante pulled on the boots to turn a circle, so Carlos's head was north.

'Turn him over!'

Carlos. Not heavy. Speed freak. His blood not liquid now?

Lily had shot a white man. He'd come to steal her favorite horse, just to mess with her, and she shot him. Buried him under the corral.

Dante knew this asshole would shoot him as soon as the body was in the Ranger. He pulled the boots a few inches, onto the old pitted asphalt, and the body sighed. Carlos sighed. He dropped the boots. Carlos's back, onyx skin under ragged holes in the green jacket, rose and fell. Carlos was breathing. Dante backed away. The guy lowered his gun and walked toward Carlos.

Dante's father stepped out from the side of the house and fired the rifle from there. Thirty feet. The tranquilizer dart hit the man in the shoulder blade. Something flew from his mouth and landed in the sand. The gun dropped and he fell to his knees.

Dante ran over and slid a fat splinter of dried palm frond behind the trigger, carried the gun to his father. He picked up the flashlight and trained it onto the other thing in the dirt. Top teeth – a pink-and-white clamshell in the dirt.

'Fuck,' the guy shouted, clutching for the dart he couldn't reach, the blood bright red between his fingers. 'You –' he said.

Dante's father crouched near the guy and said, 'Call me that and I'll shoot you in the nuts, man. Just to hear you scream. I will tranquilize your scrotum.'

His father's hair glistened with sweat in the starlight, his T-shirt wet and transparent over his chest. The pouches under his eyes triangular. Like viper heads. Five puppies, he'd said when he got home at midnight. The mother hit by a car. Musta been half-dead and she tried to crawl back. I had to look forever to find her. By the freeway.

His father had been asleep for only two hours when the power went out. His eyes were slitted and golden.

'Are you fuckin' serious?' the man moaned. He was crumpling, fading.

His father stayed crouching near the man and said softly, almost tenderly, 'Shut your punk ass up. You know how hard it is for me not to shoot the next dart into your eye? You made my son touch that guy. You put that in his head?' The knot of bandanna jaunty over the white man's neck. 'Oh, you a Fake Crip? You know how hard it is for me not to bury your ass under the corral?'

'The other one's alive,' Dante said.

'Damn,' his father winced. He got up and looked at Carlos in the flashlight beam. The skull. The trail of his hips through the sand. 'Get your phone and call Uncle Perry. He had to hear the rifle. Then call 911. Tell them we need an ambulance. Tell them it's Grief and ask if Tyrone's on duty.'

The white man was out now. An animal.

Dante started to walk up the path to the house, light from the sieve of sky on the white stones. His father whistled absentmindedly. Five notes. Snowflakes on mittens. Dante fell onto the cement and cried. Blown sand cutting into his cheek. His father crouched beside him then and whispered, 'The Leonids come in November, right? It'll be dark and I'll sit out here with you.' ■

Sandar Valiulin, the author's father, *c.*1955
Courtesy of the author

ROOT AND BRANCH

Sana Valiulina

TRANSLATED FROM THE RUSSIAN BY POLLY GANNON

After the October Revolution of 1917, people in Russia could no longer travel freely. This did not mean, however, that people lived peaceful, settled lives. On the contrary, tumultuous currents of humanity began crisscrossing the Eurasian plains. Movements of various army troops, paramilitary formations of peasants cut off from their land, foreign legions, workers and skilled craftsmen, and roving bands of every political persuasion merged and intertwined with countless refugees fleeing chaos and death. The death throes of the old empire lasted from 1918 to 1922, in a civil war costing Russia tens of millions of lives. Two million people, with or without family jewels, managed to make their way to Europe.

Even after the country had more or less set itself to rights again, traveling was not easy. The Soviet rulers were suspicious of the unregulated movement of citizens. A person who moved about freely could pick up free ideas, threatening state security. Moreover, the new empire had two grand aims: industrialization at the fastest possible rate, and the re-education of class enemies – which potentially included all citizens. These two goals coincided in remarkable ways, generating new flows of people. Thus, one segment of the population transported another one: prisoners destined for corrective labor camps and forced to work on large-scale socialist construction projects. In maps of the north-east, the Gulag and construction project sites were indistinguishable.

The Second World War intensified the massive movements of people. Many more were arrested and deported, others were mobilized. Millions of civilians were evacuated or fled to the east or to the west. From a bird's-eye view, the currents of humanity resembled long, turbid rivers that cut across the face of the Earth, which had grown old and disfigured before its time.

Sometime around 1943, in the middle of this human maelstrom, a young girl, along with her mother, her sister and two brothers, set out westward, fleeing from the war. At about the same time, the Germans were transporting a young Soviet prisoner of war, destined, probably, to help build the Atlantic ramparts. It was not the first time their lives were hanging by a thread. Nor were they even close to meeting. Because the current my father was caught up in was more or less continuous with my mother's trajectory, though the distance that separated them was at least 1,200 kilometers, they could not have intersected. They would have to wait three years to learn of one another's existence, and another nine before they finally met face-to-face.

In one of his interviews, Joseph Brodsky said that after the death of our parents we become consequences without an initial cause. We find ourselves in an existential void from which we have been shielded by the simple fact of their existence. How is one to cast a charm over this void, or fill it up, in order to recover one's connection with the world and move forward in it? How does one rediscover the cause? Most likely by learning to know one's parents again, this time as children of their own parents, and children of their time.

I first tried to understand my parents' life and fate after my father's death. This was a professional, somewhat mercenary, interest, as I was preparing to write a novel about them. I intended to weave a narrative from facts, filling the gaps with my own imaginative efforts. Since the events in the novel take place before my birth, when my parents were not yet my parents, I could unleash my imagination.

Writing about my father means writing about my mother – and vice versa. Indeed, if it hadn't been for a letter that she wrote to him in 1946 while he was in the Gulag, before she had ever laid eyes on him, I would not have existed. After the camps, my father was banned from living in Moscow – his birthplace – as well as from other large cities in the Soviet Union. Their first meeting took place in 1955 in Moscow and turned out to be a great disappointment to my mother. My father didn't look like the romantic hero she had created in her imagination. But they married, and he went to live with her in Tallinn, where she had fled to from Leningrad in 1943 after having lost her parents. Their fates were still tightly bound up with history itself – its 'iron will', as Marxist-Leninists might have put it.

I am writing about my father, but I don't want to lose sight of my mother. She will be my guide and my guardian angel, as she was in life; as she was to my father during their nine-year-long correspondence. 'While faithful eyes cry with you, this life is worth the suffering,' he wrote to his 'faraway and close friend', citing Schiller in one of his few letters from the Gulag that have been preserved.

The trajectory along which my father moved from 1941 to 1955 – or, rather, the current that swept him up – begins in Moscow and veers off toward the south-east, to the city of Engels on the Volga, where he was taught to shoot and parachute-jump. As part of the paratroopers division, my father flew from Moscow to the Smolensk region, toward the strategic rear of the German army. The paratroopers drank away their fear before skydiving into the enemy's den. They jumped, machine guns at the ready, engaging in battle alongside the partisans.

In the spring of 1942 my father was wounded and taken prisoner. After this he disappeared into the enormous flood of prisoners of war in Nazi custody. For two years, his relatives lost all trace of him as he moved west through Byelorussia and Poland, through reception centers, collection points and transit camps where the prisoners were filtered. Commissars, Jews, Cheka officers and border guards were executed. The ones who survived ended up in the *Stalags* (prisoner-of-war camps). Of the cohort of boys born, as he was, in 1922, 70 to 80 per cent perished in the war. But my father survived, moving further west, to the Atlantic coast, most likely already part of the Todt Organisation, a military engineering group using forced labor.

Twelve years ago I came across a blurry photograph of my father on the pages of the American magazine *Yank, the Army Weekly*. I was in Bayeux, at the Memorial Museum of the Battle of Normandy. In the picture, my father, Corporal Sandar Valiulin, is surrounded by American officers. He is writing a flyer, urging his fellow prisoners of war to surrender. He is in the town of Portbail on the Cotentin peninsula. How did he get there? What happened to him? He never told us about it. But now, sixty years after the events, the article 'About the Russians in Normandy' tells his story, or at least a part of it. During the siege of Smolensk he was captured by the Germans and thrown in prison, where he was fed just enough to keep him alive. His fellow captives were ill and dying from hunger and lack of medical treatment.

Then, when all seemed hopeless, their captors offered them a chance to join one of their voluntary organizations. It was either that or forced labor. The people who joined were brought to Normandy and put to work digging gun emplacements and building barricades. One day he was put into a German uniform, given a rifle and told that he must fight for the 'Fatherland'. With the muzzles of his captors' guns constantly in his back he felt he had to obey, but two days after the troops' arrival at the front, he saw his chance. When none of the German officers were around he and his friend Ivan started down the railroad track which he knew led into the American lines, until they reached the road. And there they stood, two bedraggled figures waving white flags at the approaching jeep with two American medics aboard, who picked them up.

It was estimated that a total of 200,000 Russian soldiers came to France after 1943. Until September 1944, all Russian prisoners captured in the north of France, including my father, were shipped to camps in Britain. One of the few things he told me about this experience was that the NKVD officer who visited the camp to persuade them to return to Russia had been shooed away.

But after the Yalta Conference in February 1945, all Soviet prisoners of war were forcibly repatriated to Russia. My father told us that some of the prisoners in the camp committed suicide to avoid repatriation. As George Orwell put it in his reports: 'Many [Russian prisoners] seemed to feel, however, that after having served in the German Army, even though forcibly conscripted, they would be treated as traitors by the Russians and probably shot. Others appeared as resigned as ever to a fate that had long ago removed any element of choice in their lives.'

From England my father was transported by boat, first south to Gibraltar, then eastward through the Mediterranean toward Odessa. After that his route continued east, by way of Moscow, to Ufa, where, on 29 June 1945, the Military Tribunal of the Southern Ural Region sentenced him according to article 58-1B (treason of military personnel) to ten years in prison, with disenfranchisement of five years, specifically for working as a translator in a prisoner-of-war camp.

The next stop was Nyrob, a settlement on the River Kolva. Of the ten years of my father's sentence, four would be spent here.

I am traveling through the Perm region. I am not a historian, not an expert on the Gulag, and for now I am no longer even a writer. For some reason words sicken me – words that tame resistant subject matter and fashion it into a product for mass consumption. I am my father's daughter, a former prisoner of war and 'suspicious person' who spent ten years in the Gulag. I am following his footsteps, tracing his path, in a Hyundai van. I have not been to Russia for a long time, and I have never traveled so deep into the interior. All around me is a vast green emptiness. A grey sky presses down on this expanse, broken up by myriad bodies of water with names ending in '-va', meaning 'water' in the local language of Komi – Usva (Noisy water),

Kosva (Small water), Kolva (Fish water), Vilva (New water). From time to time, a cemetery springs up out of nowhere along the road. Around every grave there is a low blue wrought-iron fence. On top of the graves are plastic flowers in gaudy colors. The grass grows high between the fences, as if to discourage visitors from honoring the dead.

I am following the tracks of my father, who passed this way seventy-two years ago. But somehow I'm reminded of my childhood, of Tallinn, Estonia, and the feeling that Russia evoked in me then. The country seemed to loom over our little republic like a huge shadow. Even the sun had to struggle to shine through it. And on dull, overcast days like this one, Russia swallowed up all the last rays of light and plunged the Earth into darkness. The shadow originated in the mysterious location east of the town of Narva on the Estonian-Russian border. The next station was Ivangorod. I traveled by the Tallinn–Moscow night train when I was young. The journey brought me out of my familiar Estonian microcosm into this shadowy space, and my heart faltered. I realized immediately that different laws applied here, laws that superseded the banal physical laws of the human body. It was as if an enormous centripetal force was pulling me in, depriving me of self-awareness and self-knowledge. The train wheels were clacking and I became a silent part of some collective whole, and dissolved into it. Beyond the train was some sort of primordial substance, protoplasm, the very *apeiron* or 'boundlessness' which the ancient Greeks posited as the first principle and element of all existence, and which they feared. Indeed, the boundless whole, the indeterminate, the irrational and unpredictable, can assume any form. But the form – or *peras* – that it takes depends on human beings, and therein lies the possibility of salvation.

The Perm region is a country of exiles. It abounds in rivers and lakes; penal colonies and unbearably red sunsets; Stalinist labor camps and mighty elks, the maternal source of all the Finno-Ugric peoples; marvelous ancient and modern churches; poisoned yellow rivers and huge ancient boulders; copper, salt, coal and diamonds; wooden idols and forgotten people; abandoned mines and pangolins from the Paleozoic era; monocities built around dying industries; caves where the 'pale-eyed folk' of Finno-Ugric legend hid away from the Cossack chieftains in the sixteenth century. Here, at the eastern foot of the Ural Mountains, runs the boundary between Europe and Asia. A concrete obelisk stands on two continents, surrounded by a mountain of garbage and empty champagne bottles. Cows are grazing in the semi-mythical capital of the ancient Urals, or Great Permia, established on seven hills, like Rome. A curly haired angel, defying death and guaranteeing eternal life, hovers over the sign of a funeral parlor bearing the name RESURRECTION. Beavers gnaw through trees that topple onto electrical wires, causing frequent outages.

Here, one sees wooden figures of Christ languishing in a dungeon before his crucifixion – a favorite subject of the local craftsmen. This Christ has the angular face, narrow eyes and high cheekbones of the local Komi-Permyak people. Boris Pasternak emerged from a spiritual crisis here, having seen the light of literature. Afterward, he described the city of Solikamsk under the guise of the city of Krestovozdvizhensk ('Raising of the Cross' City), in *Doctor Zhivago*. Here, the exiled Osip Mandelstam jumped out of a second-floor window of a hospital in a fit of madness, regaining his reason. Viktor Astafiev, who ended up in this city after the Second World War, shook hands with the only person he knew there – the statue of Vladimir Lenin on the square by the railway station. And here, according to legend, a certain peasant decided to save the world by carving 500 wooden sculptures of Christ. He only managed to complete half the quota by the time he died, and so the world was not saved after all.

Rocking like a boat on the waves, the Hyundai swerves around the potholes in the road – where there are any roads to speak of. All the post-revolution settlements with Russian names – Ryabinino, Lobanikha, Krasnovishersk – were built by deportees: Germans from the Volga and 'prosperous' peasants, 'kulaks' of the second category. The kulaks of the first category were sent straight to prisons and labor camps. From the window of the van I see new brick churches among the dark gray apartment blocks of Soviet civilization. Billboards and signs exhort the locals to make a contribution to the cause of the true faith – the higher truth, they call it. The streets are still Soviet: Communist Street, Pioneer Street, Builders Street, Victory Day Street, one after another . . . They look cheerless and forsaken. What was it the Zen master asked the pupil who was searching for eternal truth? 'Have you had breakfast?' 'Yes.' 'Then go wash your plate.' Here they don't like washing plates. Perhaps it's too lowly a task, unworthy of the higher truth.

In-between the towns and settlements, new and ancient, is the taiga. We get out of the van to stretch our legs. The earth is covered in gray moss. There are countless birch trees, and a monumental stillness reigns. But from the depths of the forest, from the sky, from the rivers and from the mountains, the backbone of Russia, comes a cold existential breeze. It is unmistakable, a uniquely Russian phenomenon, untranslatable into any language. It extinguishes self-awareness and restores the natural order of existence. Here, the hierarchy of geological epochs holds sway. And yet, within this enormous expanse, it is hard to breathe – or is it the boundlessness itself, no longer just a literary paradox, that is so chokingly claustrophobic? My heart feels constricted, as it did on that night train from Tallinn to Moscow when I was a child. Who am I? But what kind of question is that? As though it had any significance at all . . . The Urals are the ideal setting for the Gulag, not only because of the abundant mineral deposits, so necessary for building a new world. Not only because there is no place to run to from here – if you try, you come up against an impenetrable wall of forests and rivers. Here, the existential breeze liberates human beings from all illusions of personhood and delivers them naked into the maw of the Gulag, the shape *apeiron* assumed in this part of the world in the twentieth century.

I have never before traveled so deep into Russia, but I recognize it, as though I am back in a long-forgotten dream. In this dream, my father is traveling under convoy on the same road our van is trundling along. His clothes are ragged, he is in a long line of others like himself, people exiled from life. The farther they travel, the more inexorably their collective suffering wipes away all individual features. His voice is attenuated, he is effaced. His fate is nothing beyond the realization of historical will. His life has no value. Like all elemental forces, history is blind. It is indifferent as to how, and when, and by whom it demonstrates its will. My father is an embodiment of the will of history. His body is raw material for the great empire. The highest meaning and purpose of his life, his individual fate, consist precisely in this, no more.

I am a bad tourist. Ungrateful. I look at the great rivers and see prisoners on barges. I look at the road and see trucks carrying people destined for the Gulag. The landscape spreads out before my eyes like a Chinese scroll, and in each unfolding image I seek my father. I look for him in clips from documentaries; I look for his photograph on the pages of Pavel Polian's book, *Victims of Two Dictators*. I look at the eyes of Soviet prisoners crazed with hunger, thrusting underwear through the barbed wire, desperate to trade it for bread. Here they are, with the same crazed eyes, gnawing at a hunk of bread, or crowding around for the distribution of their meager rations, or drinking out of puddles in the road. Here they are, assembled before a delegation of the International Red Cross, barefoot, clutching their caps in their hands, or standing with their hands behind their backs, bound to a pillar at the camp Golgotha. Their faces are tiny blurry spots, no bigger than the heads of pins in the human sea of one of the camps. As if it were possible to discern even a single face here! Again and again I peer through a magnifying glass at the face of a captive soldier, blackened by the sun. He, too, is tied to a pillar and to barbed wire; like my father, his eyes are deep-set and hollow, his nose prominent, he has long straggly white hair. The expression on his face is the same as that of the Perm Christ in the dungeon. I am familiar with this gaze from the labor camp photographs of my father – this is how the inmates from the Gulag look. They are made faceless by collective suffering. The image of the soldier unnerves me, it won't leave me in peace; but my father is no longer alive, and I have no one else to ask, no one who can tell me whether the photograph is him or not. I will have to learn to live without peace.

W e get out of the van to take in the magnificent views, the ancient churches and bell towers, icons, wooden architecture, colorful tiled Dutch stoves in the mansions of the nobility. We are inducted into the secrets of salt production, coal and diamond mining, and the Permian geologic period. With our cameras, smartphones and tablets we eagerly absorb all that is beautiful, eternal and good. We aren't allowed to get distracted. We are working, we can't neglect or overlook a single detail. I take picture after picture, assiduously, along with everyone else. Hundreds upon hundreds of snapshots – the same carved window frames, notched, zigzag cornices, elegant arcs and arches, saintly countenances, gilded iconostases from various perspectives and in different kinds of lighting. The snapshots impose boundaries on the boundless, they enchant us and shield our eyes and hearts from the *apeiron*. And here, on an icon, is a full-length figure of the famous St Christopher of Perm, with the face of a hound. He is the patron saint of hunters, trappers and fishermen. According to legend, a beautiful youth asked God to protect him from women by conferring on him the face of a dog, which God saw fit to do. I put down my camera and examine the saint. Christopher, with the profile of a dog's head, is a copy of the ancient Egyptian Anubis, who had the head of a jackal and was the deity of burial and embalming, and the conductor of souls into the kingdom of the dead. Later, the Greeks combined Anubis with Hermes, another conductor to the underworld, giving the hybrid-being the name Hermanubis and refashioning him with a dog's face rather than a jackal's. Anubis-Hermanubis made a long journey, but he knew where he was going, and definitely what he was doing, transforming himself into St Christopher. How hard he would have to work, conducting all those children of men who perished here in the Gulag, leading them through the 20,000 rivers and lakes of Perm into the next world! I look at the saint, and all that is beautiful, eternal and good recedes ever further from me, into the shadows of the Perm forest.

The mysteriously poetic term 'Gulag Archipelago' penetrated my consciousness in the mid-seventies. I first heard it on my father's massive transistor radio. He leaned over it with his whole body, trying to catch his portion of truth, broadcast in an easterly direction every evening by Voice of America and Radio Freedom through the crackle and static of jamming. The new words sank into my imagination along with other romantic names, like Babylon, Urartu, Illyria, Assyria, Dardania . . . I had no idea what it meant, but I hesitated to ask my father. And with some sort of sixth sense I understood that it was strictly forbidden to utter the word 'Gulag' outside home.

I have a strange father, different from the other fathers. In the first place, he is old, old enough to be my grandfather. Second, he's seen Notre-Dame de Paris, he has picked blackberries by the side of the road in France and he has been to England. Third, interesting friends of my father's sometimes visit us from Leningrad and Moscow. They have a secret that somehow links them all together, but they don't talk about it. Still, these friends curse the Soviet authorities, openly and cheerfully, and every year on 5 March, they celebrate the anniversary of the death of Stalin. My father also curses the Soviet authorities; that's fourth. Everyone dreams of going to England or to Paris, but only the bigwigs get to go. When I ask him about how and when he ended up there, he hums and haws, then changes the subject.

My father never ever throws anything away. The cupboards and drawers are stuffed with scraps of twine, old shoelaces, candle stubs, empty ballpoint pens, matchboxes and bent nails. Sometimes Mama secretly clears out the cupboards and drawers, and then there's a big row at home. My father can sulk in silence for days on end, not paying any attention to us. His face is like a dark sky before a thunderstorm and we're afraid to talk to him. We wait until the sky clears. Sometimes he explodes in thunder and lightning, Mama cries and I comfort her. Then his face brightens up again. He jokes sweetly and declares his love for her in funny Estonian. He has a round scar on his chest and a gleaming Order of the Red Star in a flat box. He's a war veteran, but on Victory Day he never goes to the big meeting of veterans.

Soon I find out from my sister, who was told and sworn to secrecy by a cousin, who in turn was told and sworn to secrecy by his freethinking mother, that Father had done time in the camps. My parents were keeping the skeleton in the closet to protect us: under Brezhnev, Stalin's labor camps were a forbidden topic. So the magical formula, the 'Gulag Archipelago', turned out to be just the Gulag, a prosaic, bureaucratic term. But for me, the Gulag was not just the name of the main administrative bureau of the labor camps. For me it was also the oppressive silence of my father, his capacity to close up for days on end, and his loneliness, which neither my mother nor I, or my sister could ever lessen or counter. It was his dark face like the color of the sky before a storm, it was his flashes of rage when all the pain and humiliation inflicted on the 'little man', the man of no consequence, poured out. Now I know why he creeps over to the radio to listen every evening. He wants to know who he is, and what happened to him and to his country. Now I know why Estonians don't consider him to be an invader, an occupier, the way they view other Russians, even though he speaks Estonian poorly. Of course, Father is a tactful and civilized man; but the main thing is that he came back 'from over there' and this, more than a common language and culture, connects him, a Russian-speaking Tatar, with the Estonians, who were also banished 'over there' or lost their loved ones 'there'. And now I know why he doesn't like the 9 May, Victory Day. It transports him, in his mind, to 'that other spring' Solzhenitsyn wrote about in *The Gulag Archipelago*, the state's betrayal of its own people.

On both sides of the road the forest is screened by high blank walls. Barbed wire twists and circles along the top of the walls. Behind the walls there are watchtowers and barracks. We are approaching Nyrob, the 'end of the world'. The plethora of Gulag camps has dwindled now to three correctional penal colonies. Seventy-two years ago, when the current swept my father to this place, the Nyrob Labor Camp consisted of thirteen auxiliary camps next to a large-scale Gulag logging operation. I don't know which camp my father was in. He, and the other prisoners like him who had spent time in Europe, had to be isolated from society so as not to corrupt the innocence of ordinary Soviet citizens.

We are on our way to look at the famous Nikolsky Church. It is not simply a beautiful five-cupola structure from the seventeenth century, baroque and lacy, like a great sailing ship seen from afar. It is a wonder church, a miracle of the true faith. According to legend, it was built by mysterious craftsmen: 'no one knew where they came from, or who hired them'. It was built without the use of scaffolding or platforms. Every day they would build and every night the church would sink into the ground. The next morning they would start to build again. Then the master craftsmen suddenly disappeared and the next morning the church rose up, as it stands today. The wonder church was built on the order of Nikolai the Wonder-worker. His icon appeared three times on the stump of a tree, our priest of the true faith tells us, to which it kept returning miraculously from the neighboring Cherdyn, until it was understood that the hand of the Almighty was at work, and that a church was to be built exactly on this spot, where 'all roads end'. Our priest also heaps criticism on the internet and bemoans the erosion of morals; but he is kindly disposed toward us. Dressed in the garb of pious wayfarers, we sit on benches, our hands folded in our laps, and listen to him talk about the martyr Boyar Mikhail, uncle of the first Romanov, whose body, after being buried in the ground for five years, remained intact and uncorrupted, except for two fingers on one of his hands. People touched the fetters of the saint to cure themselves of ailments. The priest is indignant about the Komsomol members from the Militant Union of Atheists, who threw garbage into the martyr's grave in the 1930s. I think about the tens of thousands of convicts who felled trees here to fulfill Stalin's five-year economic plans. Almost nothing is left of the camps now. Nature is encroaching. Besides, the disintegrating labor camps of the Gulag do not fit into the program of the beautiful, eternal and good. There is nothing to see here; and so, why talk about something so sad, why rub salt into our wounds? As it is, everything is already so clear, so obvious. Evil is an unavoidable, fundamental part of existence. Like the mighty forces of nature that surround us, it always was and always will be. In the country of the Gulag they prefer not to recall the Gulag.

But in the labor camp museum you can witness the construction of this earthly hell. People who say that Russians are lazy and disorganized are wrong. Out of the *apeiron* that spread throughout Russia after 1917 they fashioned prisons and labor camps, and filled them with people. The ordinariness of the facilities of hell on earth, their banality, is striking. Those who doubt the words of Hannah Arendt should visit the Museum of the History of Political Repression Perm-36 (also known as the Gulag Museum) to see how right she was. Here, there is not even a hint of Dante's hell. It reminds me of Dostoevsky's idea of eternity in *Crime and Punishment*. The cells are reminiscent of a rural bathhouse, a smoky space with spiders lurking in the corners. But the world of the Gulag is terrible not only in its banality but also in its ubiquitousness – and, therefore, in its ineradicability. This is a world turned upside down, where notions of truth, love and goodness, inherently pliant and ambiguous terms, become tainted and specious. Deceit reigns here; it isn't a deviation from the norm, however, but the norm itself. The Gulag is the material embodiment of deception in all its infernal essence. Satan, the father of deceit, inspired this system, changing his mask – Lenin, Dzerzhinsky, Trotsky, Stalin . . . The system was constructed and maintained by his innumerable servants, ordinary men and women who innocently believed the specious words. The lies of the Gulag were revealed, but the ethical signs or meanings, twisted and distorted in the interests of historical necessity, have yet to be put right.

This is the reason why so many victims of the Gulag, including my father, felt themselves to be 'suspicious persons' even after their amnesty and rehabilitation. This is the reason why people don't want to recall the Gulag in the country of the Gulag. This is the reason why those who are trying to memorialize the camps and remember the faces of the prisoners are finding it ever more difficult to accomplish this task, and why they meet with ever more resistance.

After the Gulag Museum, the world outside seems bright and marvelous. Even our dilapidated South Korean van has recovered its spirits and speeds along the road, relieved to be overtaking the ghosts of the past. The passengers in the van have also become more lively, taking snapshots of the sun-drenched landscape through the windows with renewed energy. The human being and the machine observe a great law of life: don't look back, whatever may have happened, and keep going, up the mountain where the beautiful, eternal and good await you. The landscape is, indeed, very beautiful . . . The Perm region is called the heart of Russia. It lives up to its name. Here, far from the lights of the big city, amid the powerful cycles of nature and on the ancient breeze that extinguishes self-awareness, the past and the present of Russia swirl and merge. In a single, circular motion, pagans and Christians, exiles and industrialists, revolutionaries and priests, merchants and convicts, communists and monks, peasants and soldiers, intellectuals and laborers, prisoners and convoy guards, victims and executioners, monarchists and patriots, politicians and pilgrims, businessmen and the unemployed spin and flow together, forming a charmed circle, outside of time, where everything repeats, and from which, it seems, there is no exit. I am traveling through the timeless heart of the empire. Soon I will leave this region and the current that swept my father along seventy-two years ago, but it will remain inside me. Like Russia, I am, for the time being, unable to break this vicious circle, to escape this devil's dance. ∎

MALL CAMP, SEASONS 1 & 2

Joshua Cohen

I t was a massive commercial structure outside Kavala, Greece, with spalled concrete walls and a collapsed concrete roof and all of its interior so smashed up, trashed, without utilities and ruinous that when his boatload of refugees was first apprehended and brought here, his parents had burst into tears. They thought the war had been here too. They thought the war had been here before them.

The war was everywhere, inescapable. Like the barbed-wire fence that surrounded the parking lot. Like the guards who patrolled the fence.

The truth, however, was that the destruction here wasn't from fighting, but from a crisis of global economy. This place his family was being forced to live in now was a mall, or was planned to have been a mall, but then the world's financial markets crashed, the bank loans fell through, construction was halted, and the building was left incomplete. It was left to the whims of the state that seized it and to the EU, UN, sundry NGOs and the seasonal devastations of the weather.

Parts of the mall were one floor tall and parts of it were two floors tall, but most of it was something crumbling between. At the center of the building was an atrium of escalators stilled into stairs and a squat metal information kiosk whose panes were shattered and lacked a map.

He was thirteen years old or just about and newly an only child. Newly not a child. He'd been growing out of everything: his shyness, his stammer, his donated sneakers and donated sweats – all of him expanding like the hallways into mystery.

The hallways were lined with storefronts, or what were supposed to have been storefronts, each given over to a single family initially, so that in the early days, the families that'd fled together lived together, whether next door or along the same forlorn stretch of cracked LED lighting and patchy tile.

But later, as more arrivals kept coming, families were compelled to make space in their storefronts to accommodate the unstoppable influx of uncles, aunts, cousins and unrecognizable friends, so that even while the hallways were becoming more cramped, they were also losing the only characteristics – the scents, dialects and sanguinary ties – that had ever made them feel familiar and distinctive.

The hall his family was on was still, to a degree, one of the proud old Aleppo halls, though it was swiftly becoming one of the major Homs halls too, even while its farthest reaches were being colonized by boorish tribes from the rural Hauran, with the terminal vestibule converted into the slovenly redoubt of the Abazaid clan.

This diversity meant that the hallways presented differently – they presented different privileges, prospects and hassles – depending on who you were or were related to or what city or province you'd fled from. It was also why no one could ever agree on what to call them. The only universal toponyms were Red Hall, Green Hall, White Hall and Black Hall, the gates to which still retained traces of red, green, white and black paint. That color scheme hadn't been extended to any of the other hallways, however, so that what his parents called Brick Hall (because of all the spare bricks that'd been there, before they were scavenged), his uncle called In-Law Hall, and his aunt called The Hall In Which I Can Finally Sleep Undisturbed.

Because of the overcrowding in Brick Hall, his uncle and aunt moved in here and divided the storefront with him and his parents.

Their areas were separated by tarpaulins hung from a pipe and held down by bricks.

Arguments were common. Since the arrival of his uncle and aunt, he'd been avoiding spending time there. He'd wander the NGO corridors. Bumming candies and gums. Sitting on the sidelines of football matches. He'd pretend to search for his sister, who'd died with her husband's family in an airstrike in Damascus. He'd invent rendezvous with imaginary friends. He'd volunteer for errands.

His parents, his uncle and aunt would send him out on errands to Liberty Square, al-Azizia, beyond – to Idlib, Hama, Palmyra – to halls they'd call by contradictory names or only describe to him, but in ways that were constantly changing, like the halls themselves were constantly changing, like he changed.

His thoughts, his words, his accent.

The directions would be: find the dry fountain and count two storefronts down. Keep going until you reach the wiring repurposed into clotheslines. Make a left by that crazy lady who feeds the pigeons. Make a right past the last window of the Melkites that still has its glass. Ask for a man named Hafez. Who'll recognize you. Ask for a man named al-Noury. Who's the cousin of the husband of your sister.

He was never sent to return something borrowed without borrowing something else. He was to deliver the requests and accept what was given, all with pleasant deference, which was even how he'd accept the refusals.

He had to stay focused, on task. Focused on what his parents wanted (flameless cooking fuel, which were sometimes labeled 'hexamine tablets' and sometimes labeled 'esbits'). Focused on what his uncle and aunt wanted (scissors). He had to keep repeating the messages to keep them straight. Repeating them mentally, repeating them aloud, as the scenery looped, the routes became tangled. Each turn he took, there'd be another face. Each concourse held a voice, importuning, beckoning.

His one regular daily trip was to the Red/Green spigot for water. He'd be carrying a jug. Carrying it empty there, full back. Light then heavy.

He'd take the Red route there, the Green route back, until a ceiling caved in and blocked the Red and the elders of the Green commandeered the hose.

He had to find other spigots.

There was one in the Hospital, down past the cubicles of the blue-jacketed medics. There was another in the Office of Documents, behind the cubicles of the bluejackets who spoke a passable Arabic and helped with translating, interpreting, filing forms. Though it was never very obvious: which was the line for medical aid, which was the line for legal aid, and which was the line for water.

Yet another spigot was outside by the loading docks, where every moon or so a man who'd smuggled an ancestral blade over the border to Turkey – who'd smuggled it through Turkey and onto the hell boat to Lesbos – unsheathed that blade and pronounced God's name and slit the throat of a goat.

S tores started opening in the storefronts: people got ahold of basic ingredients and cooking equipment from the bluejackets and even from the guards and started to cook. Someone got ahold of some cobbling tools and began a business mending shoes. His family's storefront became a combination kitchen – which supplied a cafe collectively improvised among the remnants of the mall's food court – and tailor shop. His mother did the cooking, his aunt did the tailoring. Because so few people had money, and what money was had was so precious and hoarded, most of the transactions were trades. Barters. Goods for goods. He'd be sent out to a certain theater of 'the multiplex movie theater', to a certain lane of 'the bowling alley', to the only elevator that was still an elevator on The Way of Open Shafts, carrying a skirt or blouse of rags, a shawl sewn together out of Chinese tartan totebags and Russian nylons, a cardboard box of kibbeh seeping soy grease, or a broomstick threaded through the warped holes of unleavened ka'ak – carrying instructions too, in his head, about what to expect, what to demand, in return. Money, always start the bargaining with money. Take bills, even coins. Not the ones with Arabic on them. The ones without Arabic. If they don't have any bills or coins, or if they only have the ones with Arabic, take soap and razors. Take frying oil too. Not used frying oil. New. Soy before palm. Palm before canola. The people he had to deal with, even the cousins he had to deal with, would try to stiff him, by claiming his parents had debts. They'd try to take what was offered at no cost. Taking what was owed them. They'd give him soap clumped together from bits of bars. Hairs would still be stuck to them. The razors would be dull, jagged, spattered. The new oil would just be old oil, inadequately strained, and once he was hauling a load of it back to his parents in a repurposed spackling pail and the handle snapped and the pail fell to the floor and the oil it spilled was filthy with charred chickpeas. He ran back to his hot kitchen storefront crying and forgot the bucket. His mother stopped his father from smacking him. His mother smacked him herself.

It was about this time that a real store opened up in the atrium. A real store owned by real foreigners, who came and went every day and didn't live inside it.

The store accepted, as its sign stated, real money only: €, $, ₺.

VIP was its name and he went there with his father and when his father had to help his mother, he held their spot in line.

He held their spot in lines, because each hallway had its own line slightly longer than a day – all of the lines braiding together into a single line only in the atrium, where everyone jostled. He had to use his elbows, he had to use his shoulders. He waited through the night, even after the VIP had closed, alternating shifts of sleep with his father. When the VIP reopened, it emerged that the dozen or so people still ahead of them had been holding spots for relatives who only now were cutting in and so everyone behind was yelling and shoving, in a tumult that was interrupted by the morning call of the muezzin and then continued, in a different vein, when those who didn't pray insisted on the privilege of jumping the line ahead of those who did.

He went down on his knees in front of his father, because his

father's spine was bad, and felt for the money. The money was in his
father's shoe, stitched inside its tongue. He extracted it. Folded to the
size of a postage stamp. Damp. Turkish lira. Not quite euros, not quite
dollars, but also not quite Syrian pounds. The sum was enough for
the cheapest phone, which came wrapped like a baby in its charger.

After that purchase, the errands changed. He'd be dispatched
back to the VIP, usually weekly, to wait in line again and the wait, the
line, was only barely shorter. He'd come here, as the others who'd
already bought phones would come here, to buy the time that made
phones work. To buy the minutes, the hours, air. Refill credits, which
came on cards. After a while the atrium line was divided into two
lines – one for people buying phones, one for people buying credits –
and then after another while it was combined into a single line again.
Some weeks his parents would have him buy thirty minutes, some
weeks they'd have him buy an hour. A week became the span of the
time purchases. A week was either thirty minutes or an hour. The
money was flecked with flour and creased sweaty like his mother's
hands. He'd take the card the credits came on back to their storefront,
where his father would scrub away the metal coating – as if scouring
burnt bulgur from the bottom of a vat – to get at the numbers below.

Some conversations his father would have in their storefront, but
others required a walk. His father, cupping the phone to an ear like
a seashell, would go out walking the halls among all the other people
who were walking the halls on phones of their own – walking, talking,
cupping their free ears so as to hear better.

He'd follow at a distance, in and out of range. Past the bathrooms
with sinks but no toilets and the bathrooms with toilets but no sinks.
Around barricades of pallets. Puddles. Creeping weeds of blue
graffiti.

His father greeted the people he passed with silent nods. Violent
gestures became cursory waves. And then his father, and the people
his father knew and even didn't know, all returned to their phantom
dialogues, seething.

One walk brought his father and so him into the atrium again and to the VIP. His father waited in line. He waited on his father behind the mapless information kiosk, until the phone was fully recharged.

His father's pockets were jammed with cards.

Another walk had led up an escalator to what existed of the mall's higher floor. Twisted rebar, broken benches. Busted PA megaphones swung from their poles. Men, all men, lived together in tents under a roof that was like a tent pitching inward. A cruel dog was chained to a grating. Its collar was studded with nails.

He descended and abandoned his father, who'd always return to their storefront at too slow a pace, slow and stooped. To be interrogated by his mother. To be cursed by his mother. His father never let her touch the phone.

A new store opened up, just next to the VIP – Telekom was its name and it also sold phones and credit for phones and sessions of charging and one day a man standing outside it handed his father a hat that read TELEKOM: LIFE IS FOR SHARING and another day another man canvassing the atrium handed his father a shirt that read ONE LIFE – ONE LOVE – ONE VIP and his father gave him the hat – which was too big for the boy even with its brim tucked in – and gave him the shirt – which billowed with a supernumerary sleeve and swung at the boy's knees – so that wearing both he appeared like a wizened imam making his alms rounds in a neon yellow skullcap and dishdasha.

In a frontage across from the competing stores, there was a grocery now, which sold food ingredients and packaged food, but refused to carry the food that the people prepared themselves and sold to one another in the food court. The grocery also did a business in phone accessories like bluetooth headsets and served as a bureau of currency exchange. Inside, bracket-mounted on its back wall, was a TV, a flat screen. It was kept on constantly from open to close. To attract customers and entertain them while in line, to entertain the blonde woman who manned the counter.

He, in all his senses, was captured. Now he'd follow his father only as far as the atrium. He'd go out on errands for his mother and be detained. He'd stand outside the grocery and press his face up against its plate glass, watching. What the screen showed always changed. He wasn't familiar with anything on it. The women on the screen were, like the woman behind the counter, so unnaturally blonde it was like their hair was indistinguishable from their skin color. The one behind the counter would watch the ones up on the screen and when the shows they were in were over, she'd pick up a brick-like remote and change the channel. She never watched the news and ignored, or just pretended to ignore, any of her customers who requested it. She just put on whatever she wanted. As did the other woman with the pink-purple hair and rusty complexion who worked some days. The two women alternated. But not in any way that gave him any sense of calendar. The guy who brought the women was the same. With teeth like an extra set of keys, with a body that was a bundle of muscle. In the mornings, the guy would bring whichever of the women and unlock and raise the shutter. Then the guy would unlock the door and switch on the gas-powered generator and switch on the lights and take from his rucksack the cashbox and new inventory. Shoelaces, toothbrushes, toothpastes. Cigarettes by the carton or pack or individual. Even beers. One time the guy brought a brindled cat without a tail, which ran away.

The first show of the day was typically about the guards. About detectives. They'd find a murder in a tiny wooden bed in a tiny wooden inn or splayed out in the middle of a flowering meadow, whichever – they'd always have thirty minutes, except sometimes they'd have an hour, to find the murderer. Who usually turned out to be one of the victim's co-workers or relatives. The last show of the day depended. Whichever woman was working would click away from the news and land either on a show about nature or a show about decorating a house. But once the woman clicked away from the news to a channel showing friends, but nude friends – rough hands spreading a vagina apart as if to shape its bald dough into pastry and then a tongue dipping down to wet it or taste, just as the muscle guy came in to close, and he hurled his rucksack at the blonde woman's head, and the blonde woman – who'd been rushing to serve her last customers and hadn't noticed the programming – sobbed.

The kids – not just him but others, his age and younger – scattered through the halls. The next day, they were back against the plate glass. The rusty woman was behind the counter – the more tolerant one, who even let them inside the premises and only kicked out the older kids for shoplifting.

The blonde woman returned days later wearing sunglasses.

The boys would have to guess. They'd have to trade their guesses. About what was happening. About what was being said. Given that none of the shows were in Arabic. All they could do was project. All they could do was imagine.

He was talented at this, or his new friends regarded him as talented, because after a time they hushed their efforts and just listened to him talk. They looked at the screen but listened to him and it took just a few episodes of this for him to realize what they thought. They thought he understood. They thought he was telling them everything. All that was being said. All the dialogue. They thought he was translating, interpreting, narrating faithful sense out of the alien garble. He was ashamed. He was confused. He was happy. He did nothing to disabuse his new friends of his skill – to the contrary, he let them believe it and, on especially fluent nights, he might even have come to believe it himself: that everything was becoming clear to him.

Like Carrie. Like Rachel. That must've been their names, because the other characters kept repeating them, and whenever they said Carrie, Carrie turned, and whenever they said Rachel, Rachel turned.

The rusty woman behind the counter was Carrie. The blonde woman was Rachel. The key-toothed guy who brought them in the morning and brought them away at night was Mr Big, who kept setting the traps and collecting the traps that were killing the mice and telling him and his friends to be careful around them, because the traps were – *sma*, he said, *sma* – which neither he nor his friends understood, so Mr Big took out his phone and flashed them the Arabic word he'd found for 'poison'.

He stuck a skull decal onto the plate glass that read POISON.

One day, Rachel was at the counter with a neck brace – her eyes were still swollen and bruised like rotten apples and when he and his friends tried to venture inside, she snapped and chased them out with a mop.

One day, Carrie, who'd been getting plumper and nicer and would even now let them sit on the linoleum directly under the screen, gave him and his friends each a free chocolate egg whose hollow yolk held a toy.

Magnum (Bashar) got one with a miniature soldier. Fanta Boy (Mohammed) also got one with a miniature soldier. His held a tiny airplane.

Mr Big was the husband of Carrie, who's pregnant, and the brother or cousin of Rachel, who's unmarried and has a disease. Miranda and Phoebe were the women who worked the desks at the phone stores now and who once, on a break, took pills and snuck behind the dumpsters with the NGO workers Chandler and Ross.

During the day, when he's not at the grocery, Mr Big is at the gym. He's stuck on buses and trains. He's always checking his watch. He can never decide what to wear. Carrie leaves her wedding ring in the machine that washes dishes. Rachel has a toy that vibrates like a phone that she puts in her suitcase and brings to the airport but a guard finds it and Chandler and Ross, who'd stopped by the grocery to buy batteries and stood around watching, laughed – this was the scene they laughed at the most.

The challenge, for him, had gone far beyond just discerning the plots: now he was trying to make the plots connect, to make the plots continuous. Episode to episode. But the way life was, both onscreen and off, was frustrating all attempts in that direction. No day seemed to have any relation to the day before it or the day after it. Each day seemed like starting anew. With another minor accident or mishap amplified into a crisis, to be resolved or just forgotten by the next commercial block. Some Kurdish farmer type would stumble into the grocery bleeding from the head, caught in the grip of morphine withdrawal and a ravening madness, and yet the next time he'd notice the man, the man would be regular, healed and calm – the man would be like a different man, who'd appear to have no memory whatsoever of what'd happened and everyone here, he decided, was expected to act in that way, as if they never remembered anything.

A beggar fainted outside one of the phone stores and was ported away ringing and dripping and never returned. No one ever said anything about it.

No one ever knocked at his storefront. They just barged on in, no matter how late or how early. Cousins. In-laws. Strangers who were his parents' friends from school or work, from another life, from the life they had before. They came, they helped themselves, they made themselves at home.

Fanta Boy was here to borrow sugar. Magnum was here to borrow salt. His mother complained about having loaned her ladle out to the Abazaids, who'd loaned it out to the Hafizis or the Shamsis, who'd lost it. His aunt complained about missing some thread. His father and uncle were shrieking that a wall had just collapsed.

He hurried to the atrium. The front wall of the mall was gone. The wind was blowing in. The cold. The guards, the fence, the sky. He waded through the rubble toward the cameras and mikes, the crew whose coats read PRESS. He wondered if they would shoot him. ∎

CONTRIBUTORS

Natascha Bruce translates from the Chinese. Her current projects include *Lonely Face* by Yeng Pway Ngon and *Lake Like a Mirror* by Ho Sok Fong, which was awarded a 2017 PEN Presents award.

Edward Burtynksy is a Canadian photographer. His work has been exhibited in collections around the world, including the National Gallery of Canada, the Museum of Modern Art and the Guggenheim Museum in New York, the Reina Sofia in Madrid, Tate Modern in London and the Los Angeles County Museum of Art in California.

Brian Allen Carr was the winner of the inaugural *Texas Observer* Short Story Contest as judged by Larry McMurtry in 2011. His stories have appeared in *Annalemma, Boulevard, Fiction International, Hobart, Keyhole, Texas Review* and elsewhere. His first novel, *Sip*, was published in 2017.

Joshua Cohen lives in New York City. His books include the novels *Book of Numbers, Witz, A Heaven of Others* and *Cadenza for the Schneidermann Violin Concerto*. His essay collection, *Attention: Dispatches from a Land of Distraction*, is forthcoming from Random House in 2018. He was named one of *Granta*'s Best of Young American Novelists in 2017.

Jason Cowley is editor of the *New Statesman* and a former editor of *Granta*. He is the author of the novel

Unknown Pleasures and *The Last Game: Love, Death and Football*.

Anthony Doerr's most recent book, *All the Light We Cannot See*, won the 2015 Pulitzer Prize for Fiction and the 2015 Andrew Carnegie Medal for Excellence in Fiction. He lives with his family in Boise, Idaho.

David Flusfeder's most recent novel is *John the Pupil*. He teaches at the University of Kent. He is working on a new novel, which will be a moral thriller, and a non-fiction book about luck.

Polly Gannon holds a PhD in Russian Literature from Cornell University. She has lived in St Petersburg since 1997, where she is the director of cultural studies at the New York–St Petersburg Institute of Linguistics, Cognition and Culture.

Charles Glass has been a regular visitor to Syria since 1973. His books on the Middle East include *Tribes with Flags: A Journey Curtailed, The Northern Front* and *Syria Burning*. He was ABC News chief Middle East correspondent from 1983 to 1993.

Will Harris is an assistant editor at the *Rialto* and part of the editorial team behind *Swimmers*, a publishing project. He has published a pamphlet of poems, *All this is implied*, and an essay, *Mixed-Race Superman*. His work is also featured in the Bloodaxe anthology *Ten: Poets of the New Generation*.

Ho Sok Fong is the author of two story collections, *Maze Carpet* and *Lake Like a Mirror*, which will be published in English by Portobello Books in 2019. She is the 2016 recipient of a Taiwan National Culture & Arts Foundation grant, to support the completion of her first novel, *The Forest in Full Bloom*.

A.M. Homes's most recent book is the novel *May We Be Forgiven*, winner of the 2013 Women's Prize for Fiction. 'Days of Awe' is taken from a story collection with the same title, forthcoming in 2018 from Viking in the US and Granta Books in the UK. She teaches at Princeton University and lives in New York City.

Don McCullin is a British photojournalist, particularly recognised for his war photography in Cyprus, Egypt, Syria and Vietnam. He was the first photographer to be awarded a CBE.

Nathaniel Mackey is the author of six books of poetry, the most recent of which is *Blue Fasa*; an ongoing prose work, *From a Broken Bottle Traces of Perfume Still Emanate*, whose fifth and most recent volume is *Late Arcade*; and two books of criticism, the most recent of which is *Paracritical Hinge: Essays, Talks, Notes, Interviews*. His awards include the 2006 National Book Award for Poetry, the 2008 Stephen Henderson Award from the African American Literature and Culture Society, the 2015 Bollingen Prize for Poetry and a Guggenheim Fellowship. He is the Reynolds Price Professor of Creative Writing at Duke University.

Chelsey Minnis writes poetry and screenplays. Her fourth book of poetry *Baby, I don't care* is being published by Wave Books in 2018. She lives in Boulder, Colorado.

Gus Palmer is a documentary photographer and film-maker. He is currently working on a project in Nagorno-Karabakh, a region on the outer edges of the former Soviet Union.

Stephen Sharp is a writer living in Reading. His work has previously appeared in the *London Review of Books*.

Susan Straight has published eight novels, including *Highwire Moon* and *Between Heaven and Here*. Her memoir *In the Country of Women* is forthcoming from Catapult. 'The Perseids' is part of a new novel, *Mecca*. She lives in Riverside, California, where she was born.

Sana Valiulina is an essayist and the author of four novels. Born in Tallinn, in Soviet Estonia, she studied Norwegian at Moscow State University before moving to Amsterdam in 1989. She received the Jan Hanlo Essay Price in 2017. Her latest novel, *Not Afraid of Bluebeard*, was published in Russia in 2017. She writes in Dutch and Russian.

Not yet a subscriber?

Since 1979, *Granta* has provided a platform for the best new writing. These pages defined the literary genre Dirty Realism, tracked down a deposed South American dictator, documented the fall of Saigon, invented the Best of Young Novelists format, explored the strange world of Chinese cricket fighting, published eighteen Nobel laureates and highlighted the literary landscapes of Brazil, India, Ireland, Japan and Pakistan.

Don't miss out.

Subscribe now from £32/$48 per year.
Digital subscriptions also available from £12/$16.

Visit granta.com/takeasub for details.